THE EGYPTIAN PHILOSOPHERS:

Ancient African Voices from Imhotep to Akhenaten

MOLEFI KETE ASANTE

Chicago, Illinois

Front cover illustration by Tony Quaid
Text illustrations by Aaron Wilson
Copyright © 2000 by Molefi Asante
First Edition, First Printing

Printed in the United States of America

ISBN: 0-913543-66-7

CONTENTS

PREFACE

I have written this book for those who are interested in discovering the knowledge of the ancient ways. One does not have to possess knowledge of the Egyptian language to read this book and to benefit from the extensive wisdom of an ancient people whose civilization lasted longer than any other. It is meant for the seeker intending to uncover the earliest reflections of humanity and for the student searching for the sources of African ideas and philosophies. Therefore, this book is not written for the professional scholar, though it is hoped that all will find it rewarding. Written for the popular audience, it is essentially about the foundations of African thought and hence, of the first world thought.

This is a book about how the ancient Egyptians in Africa attempted to order their lives, heal themselves, and live with their fellow humans in an integrated society of praise and honor to the supreme deity. This book is not about the material conditions of ancient Egypt. Since there is a preponderance of works that deal with the nature of archaeological finds, the provenance of pyramids and temples, the nature of Tutankhamen's treasures, and the like, I have deliberately tried to concentrate on the intellectual and ethical gifts of the ancients. In this line of work I am following the path charted by the eminent scholar of ancient Egyptian philosophy, Maulana Karenga, who has written a major work on Maatian ethics.

The antiquity of African philosophy is unique and stands alone and is older than all other philosophies. While civilizations such as the Sumerian and Minoan produced pottery, vases, and frescoes during the period of the earliest Egyptian dynasties, only Egypt produced a body of work consistent enough in ethical, spiritual, and moral aspects to be called philosophy. It would be much later, nearly two thousand years, before the Greeks, who were influenced by the Egyptians, would develop their own philosophy.

I have found it quite remarkable to discover in the ancient Egyptian philosophies the African origins of thought and ideas. The extent to which these ancient philosophies continue to impact our own contemporary lives shows the meaningfulness of their fundamental human principles.

Quite a number of books have been published in recent years on the subject of the African Mind with the intention of demonstrating the areas where the African Mind might be delineated from the European Mind. Willie Abraham's *The Mind of Africa* remains the standard by which all others are judged. It was Abraham's intention to demonstrate the complexity of African ideas and to show that they were not simply the imitation of European ideas. He successfully argued for the unique way in which Africans responded to the universe. Other books have taken up this idea and have advanced the understanding of the ethical and social foundations of the African people.

These books have been useful. Unfortunately, they have not gone to the ancient source of the African ways of thinking: the meta-theoretical propositions and the philosophical, mythological, and mythopoetic responses Africans made to the environment, seen and unseen, and to humans, living and dead. My aim, therefore, is to introduce the reader to the earliest understandings of the human experience: birth, life, death, the good, the just, and the beautiful.

Most of what appears in this book I have delivered in public lectures, seminars, and special appearances, notably in lectures at Marquette University, the University of Iowa, and the Annenberg lectures at Howard University. However, this is a new undertaking meant to further our understanding at an elementary level about the thinking of the ancient Egyptians. I will examine the texts that laid the foundation of what is now called "traditional" in Africa and "modern" in both Africa and the West.

The contemporary world is a beneficiary of the great ideas that were developed at the very hint of history's dawn when African philosophers observed the skies, the rivers, the sun, the animals, the insects, and each other and wrote their analyses for all to learn. Out of this studied approach to human life and the environment they were able to construct protocols, meanings, concepts, ideas, and processes that have remained a part of what we do and how we think today.

We only have to look at our material and physical environment to see how greatly we have been influenced by these early Africans. Everywhere the evidences of the pyramidal form, the *tekenu* form (as in the obelisks), or the facades of buildings speak to something very ancient and deeply African. However, my purpose is not to prove any point except to introduce the reader to the wonderful joys of knowing ancient Egyptian philosophers so that their names will become as familiar to you as the names of Socrates, Plato, Confucius, Aristotle, and Mencius.

Any discussion of Egyptian philosophy must begin with a proper description of the social, geographical, and political position of Egypt within the context of Africa. Egypt is an African nation. Its history and culture during the period of its greatest achievements were intimately linked to the rest of the continent. It is not true, as Eurocentrists continue to argue, that Egypt was simply located in Africa but was really a part of the Near Eastern social reality. Some authors, such as Charles F. Aling in **Egypt and Bible History** (1992), argue that Egypt is somewhere outside of Africa. This, of course, is an anti-African viewpoint of Egyptian history and culture.

By placing Egypt in the Near East, the Eurocentrists attempt to isolate the ancient civilization from the rest of Africa. They argue that the cataracts ("impassable cataracts") prevented the Egyptians from interacting with the rest of Africa. Furthermore, they say that since the Sahara Desert was so difficult to cross, Egypt was virtually isolated from the other African nations, and thus connected to the near East. This is a patently false position which has no basis in fact; it is simply "wishful thinking" of Eurocentric scholars that creates such a misleading understanding of Egypt's place in Africa.

The cataracts in the river Nile were the first areas of portage in recorded history. Like other people in other places, the ancient Africans simply got out of their boats and carried them around the rocks. Whether the Africans were coming from the South or from the North they were able to porter their boats and equipment. Thus, the cataracts did not prevent the ancients from coming ashore. In addition, the Sahara had always been a vast area of social and economic interaction. These so-called barriers were, in fact, the real reason people were able to come together. Egypt was the place for many African cultures to come together as one. It was an amalgamation of the best that Africa had to offer.

There were several centers of learning and knowledge in ancient Egypt. Among the more select places where philosophy, commentaries on social ethics, and metaphysics were taught were the Temple of Bast at Bubastis, the Temple of Ptah at Memphis, the Sakkara complex, the Labyrinth at Fayyum, the Temple of Hatheru at Dendera, the Osirieon at Abydos, the Ramesseum, the Temple of Amen at Karnak, the Temple of Heru at Edfu, the Temple of Khnum at Aswan, the Oracle of Amen at Siwa Oasis, and the Temple of Auset at Philae. These were key centers but by no means the only sites of philosophical teaching along the Nile (Nubia had almost an equal number of high temples). The ancient Africans of the Nile Valley believed that knowledge was the way to life and the way to life led directly to the divine. Inner knowledge came from the search for the divine and wisdom was the result of inner knowledge.

An account of the earliest human thinking about the nature of the universe, human relations, good and evil, beauty, order and harmony, ethical behavior, the source of things—in effect, philosophy—brings us as close as we can get to our intellectual origins. Here I am not interested in the impact Africa had on Europe or ancient Egypt had on Greece, but rather the description and explication of the African view of reality as presented in the writings of the earliest thinkers. This departure is necessary to wrest the study of ancient Egypt from the grip of those who see it only in relationship to Greece.

Egypt is far older as a civilization of thinkers than Greece. It predates Greece not only in political terms, but in age. Egypt is thousands of years older in terms of its development of science, method, theory, and philosophy. Only when this is clearly seen and understood can we understand that Africa is the mother of all philosophy and that the ancient Nile Valley thinkers contributed to the world a full body of intellectual and creative works long before Thales, Anaximander, and Anaximenes of Miletus and Heraclitus of Ephesus, or Isocrates the Ionian came to study with them in the 6th century BC.

By the time the Greeks found Egypt, the seat of ancient wisdom and knowledge, the ancient Egyptian philosophers had been reflecting on the nature of human relationships and the meaning of life for several thousand years. Indeed, there is some indication that they had imparted their thinking, certainly in royal

viii

terms, to Crete before the explosion of Santorini. The Greeks were mere children in comparison. Nevertheless, it is important to point out exactly what the early Greeks added to the education that they received from the ancient Africans in Egypt.

The works of these early African thinkers were referred to by the Egyptian term *seboyet,* a word normally translated as "instruction" or "wisdom" and indicated a mode of discursive thinking that had its origin in the Old Kingdom. Centuries later, the Greeks wrote of these early African thinkers as *"physiologoi,"* a name they also used to refer to the Ionians in Greece who were considered observers of nature. But the *seboyet* would have most easily related to the Greek word *sophia*, wisdom. Perhaps this is why many European Egyptologists still refer to the *seboyet* as Wisdom Literature.

Inasmuch as the Greeks called their Ionians *physiologoi,* observers of nature, they demonstrated an appreciation of the system of natural observation that led to the development of science and technology in ancient Africa. Indeed, the system of observation that led to astronomy, the calendar, measurement, and medicine originated among the Egyptians.

Thales, the first of the Milesian philosophers, went to Egypt to trade but he remained in Egypt so long that he brought back to Miletus a knowledge of geometry, mathematics, and philosophy. He learned from the Egyptians the basic method for measuring land and the method of triangulation. From this basic knowledge he devised a method for determining the distance a ship was out to sea. After studying in Egypt, Thales became known as a good philosopher and an equally astute business person. He made a fortune in olive oil.

Almost all Western Classicists consider the Greek civilization to be a predecessor of Western culture. One could, however, make the argument that this is more appropriation than fact, but that is not my purpose. I would like to say that even as the Western Europeans claim ancient Greece, it remains a remarkably different society than most of Europe when you study it. One can almost make the case that Greece is closer in culture to African societies than to European. But as I have said, that is not my purpose. I only raise this to say that as we study the Egyptian philosophers, we should remember that Afrocentrists agree with Cheikh Anta Diop's claim that ancient Egypt is to Africa as Greece is to Europe. Yet we know that as all other cultures have their individuality, ancient Egyptian culture was different from the cultures of Nubia, Shilluk, Shona, Akan, and so forth. Egypt existed within the context of its own political, geographical, and mythological world. The similarities with other African societies and the Egyptian influences on other parts of Africa produced by devotees of the priests, conquests, migrations, or similar responses to the environment underscore the immensity of the debt that is owed to the Egyptian philosophers.

In 1995, I convinced African scholar Théophile Obenga of Congo-Brazzaville to join me at Temple University to teach Ancient Egyptian Language and Culture. I had studied the language myself for several years and had followed the University of Chicago's course in addition to my own work with cognate cultures in the Nile Valley. When Professor Obenga had to return home at the request of President Lissouba of Congo, I began teaching Middle Egyptian. I can confidently say that it is almost impossible to discuss, with any enlightenment, the Egyptian philosophers without some background in the classical language. It is not necessary that each reader becomes an expert but it is important to see the connection between thought and culture, between language and action, and the interaction between ideas and motifs, and so forth. Actually, I encourage the teaching of this classical African language to all African children in the continent and the Diaspora as early as possible.

One of the key Afrocentric scholars in ancient Egyptian studies is Maulana Karenga. He has produced the most detailed discussion of Kemetic ethics to date. Building on his earlier work in translating key documents into English from the Mdu Ntr, Karenga introduced the idea of a living word, a vital philosophy of the ancient Egyptians, in a way that has not been achieved by anyone else. His concentration on the social justice tradition of the ancient Africans is his intellectual gift to understanding the culture of ancient Egypt. The early work, *Selections from the Husia: Sacred Wisdom of Ancient Egypt,* was a gift to readers and scholars who had been waiting for a more readable translation of some of the important texts. Using the Old Kingdom as well as the Late Period as his chief chronological points, Karenga provides us with the words of Khunanup, Ptahhotep, Khety, and Kagemni. We are at once in the presence of the greatest philosophers of early antiquity.

Although *Selections from the Husia* is important, it is *Maat, The Moral Idea in Ancient Egypt: A Study in Classical African Ethics* that is Karenga's signature work on the ancient tradition. All future discussions of Egyptian-African ethics will be viewed in light of Karenga's shifting of the discussion away from monuments of stone to intellectual ideas. Analyzing Maat as a moral idea, Karenga shows how these principles impacted everything in the life of the Egyptian. Of course, the Sebait, the Book of Khunanup, the Declarations of Innocence, and the Declaration of Virtue, among others, are the principal books discussed in connection with Maat.

While it is not the intention of this volume to discuss the emergence of Egyptian philosophy in the common era, it should be noted that the so-called Hermetic Wisdom, attributed to a series of writings known as the Corpus Hermeticum, had a significant impact on the European Renaissance. These writings are said to be collated and collected from several African authors but usually presented as the work of the mythic figure Hermes Trismegistus—in other words, a fusion of the Egyptian and Greek cultures.

Although I shall discuss the fundamental concepts of ancient Egyptian philosophers, most of the work in this book will be devoted to the philosophers who lived well before the time usually given for the Corpus Hermeticum.

A Word of Caution

Since many of the names of the texts have been confused by earlier scholars, I shall rely on the texts where possible as the final arbiter of the names of the documents. This is necessitated by the actual texts, not by the texts that are not extant. For example, the text sometimes referred to as the "Instructions of Khety" have been called the "Instructions of Duauf" and the "Instructions of Duauf, Khety's Son." This may mean that the instructions are composed by Khety and meant for Duauf or that the instructions are written by Duauf, who is the son of Khety. The text simply says, "Instruction which a man named Duauf, the son of Khety, composed for his son, named Pepi." Although Khety is cited alongside Ptahhotep as a great scribe, it is Duauf who must be credited with the composition.

The reader will find a glossary at the end of the book which will assist with the names, events, and concepts discussed. Intended as an aid for those new to the Egyptian literature, this glossary of terms is not exhaustive, but taken alongside the bibliography, it will provide the readers with an excellent opportunity to grasp the principal elements of ancient Egyptian philosophy.

Chronology of Ancient World Philosophers

The following account of philosophers and philosophies from the most ancient times is not meant to be exhaustive but rather a way for us to have some understanding of the timeline on world philosophers. The list of Kemetic philosophers could have included Pepi, Unas, Teti, Ipuwer, and many others; however, the aim is not comprehensiveness but suggestion. Additionally, world philosophers from other cultures, such as Indian and Jewish, are not mentioned. At any rate they would not precede Imhotep, the earliest human personality.

Imhotep ca. (2700 BC)
Earliest personality recorded in history who dealt with questions of space, time, volume, the nature of illness, physical and mental disease, and immortality. There was no situation during his lifetime that did not cause Imhotep to reflect on the meaning and significance of its origin, development, and conclusion. He was the first philosopher in human history. In this sense, he is the true father of medicine, architecture, politics, and philosophy.

Ptahhotep (2414 BC)
Ancient African philosopher who produced the first ethical teaching dealing with aging. Ptahhotep was a learned priest of immense influence and power, and his instructions and philosophy have reverberated throughout the ages. With his intimate knowledge of the conditions of the noble classes and observations of the affairs of state, Ptahhotep enjoyed a special vantage point from which he saw how men held to youth even as it was fleeting. He believed that life consists of making harmony and peace with nature.

The Kagemni Sage (2300 BC)
Considered by some to be the first teacher of ethics. The Kagemni Sage sought to ensure that human beings performed right deeds for the sake of goodness rather than personal advantage. He saw good service as the object of pleasing God and believed that one must have compassion and respect for all living creatures.

Merikare (1990 BC)
Called the philosopher of communication. Merikare wrote on the value of speaking well and the importance of using common sense in human relationships. His classical teachings on good speech were recorded and passed down from generation to generation.

Sehotepibre (1991 BC)
Called "The Loyalist" by most scholars. Sehotepibre was one of the first nationalist philosophers, though decidedly royal in the sense that he believed in the rule of Kings. Sehotepibre encouraged loyalty and allegiance to the king, and often used himself as an example of one who had achieved great heights by following his own advice.

Amenemhat (1991 BC)
Thought of as the cautionary philosopher or cynic. Amenemhat was the first Kemetic philosopher who expressed a cynical view of intimates and friends, warning that a leader must be careful of those nearest to him or her. There is no evidence of a cynical philosophy prior to Amenemhat.

The Khunanup Story (2040BC)
The story of an ordinary man who is confronted by the dilemma of what to do when a rich man steals his goods. In this story,

Khunanup challenges the rich man before the magistrates and eventually wins his case. The moral lessons—i.e., the conquest of good over bad, of righteousness over evil—are remarkably contemporary.

Amenhotep, son of Hapu (1400 BC)
Next to Imhotep, Amenhotep, son of Hapu, was the most revered of the ancient Kemetic philosophers. Because of his diligence in teaching Maat, however, he became only the second teacher, after Imhotep, to be deified. He was the architect for many kings and the most knowledgeable of all philosophers of his day.

Duauf (1340 BC)
Accepted as the master of protocol. The philosophy of Duauf is concerned with the protocols of living in society. In that he urged youth to read books, he may be called the first intellectual in philosophical history. His was a remarkable testimony of the ancient African emphasis on learning. Reading was promoted as the best way to train the mind and to reveal the secrets of the hidden things.

Akhenaton (1300 BC)
Called the Father of Monotheism. Akhenaton believed that Aton was the one God. Akhenaton's choice of the small priesthood of Aton as the national religion created a massive crisis in Kemet. Soon after he moved the capital to Tell el Amarna, he was overthrown and the power reclaimed at Waset (Thebes).

Amenemope (1290 BC)
Promoted the philosophy of manners, etiquette, and success in life. Without a proverb to guide and instruct, Amenemope believed

the human being was devoid of experience and wisdom and could not learn properly. His philosophy is presented as a series of proverbs or analects that captures the knowledge and wisdom of his day. He believed that a good society was based on the proper appreciation of the ancestors since it was they who had established the proverbial wisdom.

Thales (600 BC)
Greek philosopher called the "Father of Western Philosophy." Thales studied in Africa and learned from the priests in Egypt. He then went home to Miletus and became famous as a philosopher.

Confucius (Kung Fu Tzu) (551 BC)
Responsible for molding Chinese civilization in general. Confucius exerted a great influence on the philosophical development of the concept of humanism. He turned it into the driving force in Chinese philosophy. Prior to Confucious, philosophers believed that the Way (i.e., the Tao) made men great. Confucious believed that man could make the Way great. He also believed that a good society was based on harmonious relationships. To this end he advocated a system of rules governed by virtue and moral example.

Buddha (Siddartha) (563 BC)
The royal prince who became a monk to rid himself of earthly desires. Siddartha saw four signs which led to his renunciation of the world—first, an old person, then a sick person, then a corpse being taken to a funeral, and finally a begging monk. While sitting under a banyan tree he concentrated on the ten perfections, which led to his enlightenment. Siddartha became the Buddha.

Isocrates (550 BC)
Founder of the Ionian school in Greece after he had spent years studying at Busiris in Egypt.

Socrates (480 BC)
Greek philosopher who is credited with beginning his own school of philosophy. Plato, his greatest student, recorded the wisdom of Socrates in a series of dialogues.

Mo Tzu (479BC)
Developed an ethical system based on righteousness, which he traced to the will of heaven. Mo Tzu believed that the will of heaven determined everything. Other peoples' parents and children are to be treated like one's own. This was the doctrine of moral distinction.

Plato (430 BC)
Famous student of Socrates who is often called the greatest Greek philosopher. Twenty eight of his books are extant. He recorded the dialogues of Socrates.

Aristotle (390 BC)
Student of Plato. Aristotle wrote books on rhetoric, ethics, and politics.

Mencius (371BC)
Studied with Confucius' grandson, Tzu-su. Mencius' teachings were derived from Confucius. He declared that human nature is originally good. He built his philosophy on this tenet and was the first to do so. Mencius believed that love is an inborn moral quality because man is good. Mencius insisted that the practice of love must start with the family and opposed the idea of universal love. A strong believer in political democracy, Mencius said that people had a right to revolt.

Tzu (298)

Taught the doctrine of the original evil nature of man and the necessity for its control through law and rules of propriety. Tzu believed that man could achieve goodness only as a result of his activities. His philosophy of control contributed to the authoritarianism.

CHAPTER ONE: THE AFRICAN MIND

Civilization and Culture

Suppose you walked out of your front door and looked up into the sky and instead of seeing the stars as separate entities saw them connected to each other by some visible linkage. To understand African ways of thinking it is necessary to suspend for a while linearity and to consider the entire world, even the universe or universes, as one large system where everything is connected and interconnected. This is the principal African view of reality.

The African conception of reality is often difficult for those educated in the West, or influenced by the West, where the notion of reality is so mired in empiricism dependent solely upon the operation of the senses. A further complication exists because in the West it is so easy to separate the body from the mind and one's self from others; this is a problem of concreteness and unity. In Asia the problem is different, often defying the personalism and concrete consubstantiation of spirit which is found in Africa for a more diffuse concept of spirit where nothing material exists and all materiality is an illusion. It is the giving up of the ego that is often at the core of Asian cultures; in African cultures the ego is real and materiality is concrete but manageable under the influence of custom and tradition based upon human mutuality.

Africa is a multi-plex of cultures. This does not mean that the underlying values of the various cultures are significantly different as some have tried to contend. Everywhere in Africa there seems to be, from the earliest of times, a commonality in the ways humans have approached the universe, environment, society, and the divine. It is this commonality that allows the great cultural multi-plex to be examined from the standpoint of one general civilization.

Civilization may be said to exist where a group of people or groups of people share in the same fundamental myths even though they may have different names for the experiences. Thus, in Africa it is universally held that agriculture, horticulture, and animal husbandry represent the most basic relationships one could have with the environment and the mysteries of the deities. The farmer in Mali or Senegal is considered closer to the divine than the merchant. But the same can be said for those who tend the horses in Burkina Faso, the *ouedragoes,* or the keepers of cattle among the Nuer of Sudan. On the continent, those who understand nature are considered nobler than the makers of money. One can provide numerous examples of such similarities to indicate that when we consider the ancient traditions of Africa we are dealing with the bedrock of a common civilization. Egypt, in my mind, was the most prodigious ancient civilization of Africa. Therefore, its philosophers have more to say on human relations than other civilizations by virtue of both its productivity and antiquity.

Elements of the African Mind

There are several elements in the mind of Africa that govern how humans behave with regard to reality: the practicality of wholism, the prevalence of poly-consciousness, the idea of inclusiveness, the unity of worlds, and the value of personal relationships. It is not trite for the African to say "everything is everything." And to the mind of the ancient Kemetic people this idea was thought to represent the whole universe as one. From the beginning it was the oneness of everything that became the key with which the Egyptian mind unlocked the many secrets of the world. Thus, one's world, whether from the personal or the collective perspective, was based upon the actual quest to make the world one, to establish the interconnection of all things, to reconstruct the universe as it was in the beginning.

Implicit in the idea of the beginning is the ancient view that the First Occasion represented the divine model for ordinary humans. In fact, the First Occasion must be seen as a kind of Constitution or in a more sacred sense, the Holy Scriptures, the Koran, the Torah, the Gita, or Ifa of the ancient Egyptians. Everything that happens in common time can be linked to that which happened in the First Occasion.

Such a concept was not difficult for the ancient African mind, as a similar concept, the Platonic Idea, did not seem to be problematic for the early Greeks. In the African case, however, the First Occasion was the realm of the divinities. This is not so much an abstraction as a symbolic representation of the living gods and the relationships among them. Our common experiences become indeed common because they are reflections of what occurred in the First Occasion.

As the Egyptians saw it, when God emerged from the Nun to create the universe and all things in it, including the various other appellations for the dimension and characteristics of the divine, this was the initiating of the First Occasion. This was not, though, the only thing that was to happen during the First Occasion. The divinities interacted with each other and in their relationships established patterns and behaviors that would constantly reappear in the mundane world. In the end, good will triumph over evil, although it might take a long time and many instances of conflict. As it was in the First Occasion, so it will be in ordinary time.

This process of reconnecting the world, that is, the universe as it was in the beginning, was the re-establishment of Maat. Disconnection, dislocation, and alienation were products of isfet, evil, in the world. Only through the active participation of the human mind to regain centeredness and agency could humans recapture the moment of creation.

Just as contemporary physicists are trying to understand the nature of the universe, the ancient Kemetic people tried diligently to make sense out of their world, their universe and the universes. To them, as we have now come to understand, the universe was once a tiny ball so dense that it could not be penetrated by any light and it could never release the light that it contained. Physicists tell us that it was the Big Bang that started the universes. The ancient Kemetic people understood all of this in symbolic form. Thus, when Ra created the universe, it was Ra alone from whom everything flowed. Every living thing, all forms of creatures, and all humans descended from Ra's creation. Ra was to the ancient Kemites the dense ball out of which all things were created when the Big Bang happened. Whether in the form of the supreme deity Ptah or Atum, Ra was the supreme originator because without Ra nothing that we know could have been possible. We owe even our lives to Ra's creation. The Africans believed that light itself was the creation of Ra.

Since it was the unitary Ra, that is, Ra acting alone who created the universes, nothing could exist outside of this unity. Everything has to be accounted for and all parts of the system work together like a giant puzzle. Now this is the essence of wholism; everything that is created is connected. This is the ancients' understanding of the First Time.

Just as wholism was one of the basic principles of African thought, so was poly-consciousness. Kariamu Welsh Asante has established poly-rhythmic expressions as central concepts in the understanding of African dance and musical forms. The artist can carry forth several major beats at the same time or can move several parts of the body simultaneously in a reflection of the search for harmony, which is at the end of the quest. As an expression of the numerous manifestations of African philosophy, this search for harmony, coming as it always does through movement, is another demonstration of the power of poly-consciousness.

A person may participate in poly-consciousness at several levels simultaneously. The idea is as old as the Kemetic priesthood. It was here, among the priests, where we first found that humans responded to the many levels of consciousness. Ancient priests demonstrated their ability to act at different levels, to be stimulated by many different music, and to evoke the power of the universe to assist them in their duties to the community. This idea is not to be confused with the concepts of double or multiple consciousnesses which appear in the writings of post-modern deconstructionists.

However, the mind of Africa is inclusive and can accommodate many different ideas at the same time. It is not an exclusive world that prevents other ideas from surfacing. In fact, Africans accept strangers, admit ideas, and absorb cognate cultures into their own canopy of values. The reason for this has a lot to do with the idea that everything is everything in the African view, that is, everything is related, connected, and nothing is discrete, isolated.

Ancient Egyptian philosophers were able to take the ideas that had been formed in Nubia or other African cultures and bring them into the same cosmic mythology as their own ideas. This is the fundamental reality of the philosophical approach of ancient Egypt. It is the culmination up until that time of the grandest thoughts of African people.

What is meant by the unity of worlds in the African mind is the idea that the past, present, and future are one and that it is impossible to separate them from each other. Actually, the designations past, present, and future have limited application in a discussion of the mind of Africa. These are states that are specifically geared to a Western mode of operation, whereas in Africa, the mode is orientational, perspectivist, or habitual. Human beings are oriented toward posterity. This is a perspectivist vision because it depends upon where you are in a given time and at a given point in the universe. Sometimes we are closer to the ancestors and at other times we are closer to posterity. The ancient Egyptians, like many African cultures, did not believe that the dead were disposed of forever, never to be heard of again. They were a part of our living communities, participating and acting in ways that would advance the society. Thus, when the ancient Egyptians spoke of the community, it was not simply the living but, as in other African communities, the living and the dead. When one called upon the ancestors, as in libations, it was not a simple, meaningless ceremony, but an actual invitation to the ancestors to participate and an expectation that they would surely participate if asked sincerely.

The belief in the community of the dead as one with the living community meant that there was no past, present, and future. There was only what had been done before and what would be done again. This was not to be thought of as past and future, but, rather an orientation to the whole universe, a perspective on natural and human phenomena, and an acceptance of the interconnectedness of the living with the dead and even the unborn.

Early Kemetic Concepts

One can get a fairly good understanding of the substance of the Kemetic philosophical ideas by studying some of the more common concepts that emerged in the society. Some concepts which emerged in the early Kemetic civilization were *ankh, seneb, djed, heheh, neter,* and *meri.* These terms carried powerful meanings that reiterated the notions of stability, eternity, and wellness.

Ankh is the most recognizable Kemetic glyph. It was everywhere and was used to express the idea of life, living, presence, and existence. Seneb was universally used in Kemet to represent wellness and health. Djed represented stability. Heheh was the term used for eternity. Another term used for those concepts was djet. Neter was the term used for god, the divine, or deity. Meri meant beloved or love. These concepts are often repeated in Egyptian philosophy.

In African thought positive relationships are central to the right ordering of the world. Indeed, without good human relationships the world is in perpetual crisis. One gains an appreciation of the African's concept of human centeredness in relationships by juxtaposing it to object-centeredness or other-centeredness. Relationships must begin with the interrelationship of one's personal agency in relationship to the universe and the divine. The aim then is to find the role of human agency in the reconstruction of the world as it was before the crisis of Maat and the killing of Ausar by Set.

Only the right ordering of the world through Maat can resurrect the elements of relationships that have often been dormant between humans. To the African mind it is strange that a "good" person can purchase an item for ten dollars and sell it for one hundred dollars! The person may be considered a good business person in the West, but the person is a thief to the African. How can I truly have a healthy relationship with you if I pass to you an exorbitant price tag on something for which I paid so little? So the aim of the human being must always be to establish in every relationship the conditions for Maat which include righteousness, justice, harmony, and balance. Difficulties in life can be traced to the lack of Maat in one's life. Maat is the definer of all reality.

In fact, what is clearly set forth in the works of the early Kemetic philosophers is the search for harmony in order to insure stability, which later European writers would criticize as leading to a stagnant or declining civilization. The African concentration on harmony and stability in society differed from the way the Greeks approached relationships. Pythagoras, who had studied in Egypt for 23 years, used harmony as one of his principles. He was criticized by Heraclitus who claimed that conflict, not harmony, was the true and proper state for the maintenance of the good. "Strife is justice," says Heraclitus, "...and war is the father of all."

Different African ethnic groups have used different names for Maat. For example, in the Akan tradition, the principles are as straightforward as they are among the Zulu, Yoruba, Dinka, and other African people.

The Akan believe that there are several concepts which are important in understanding how unity is achieved in the person and in the community: they are *okra, sunsum, mogya,* and *abusua.* Okra is the essence of the person, the innermost self which is often called the soul in other metaphysical systems. Okra existed in the beginning and is therefore a part of the divine nature of the human. Sunsum refers to what we have inherited as a part of the group, a sort of epic memory, or an ancestral lineage that make us who we are in a contemporary sense. Sunsum acknowledges that we are the sum total of our traditions and family members who have gone before us; we are, in fact, who they have become at this moment.

The mogya is the precise and direct relationship in a physical and biological sense that one has with the matrilineal ancestor;

it is the blood relationship. Abusua refers to one's family or community based on a physical linkage through ancestry. One's abusua is usually traced back through the mother. Kwame Gyekye has written an outstanding book on the nature of Akan philosophy in which he underscores its relationship to other African philosophies. Gyekye explains that the Akan conception of the universe emphasizes the same sense of wholism and harmony that one finds in the Yoruba culture of Nigeria or in the Zulu culture of South Africa. All are related to the ancient Kemetic conception of Maat.

The Beginning of Science

Africans were the first scientists in the sense that all science has roots in techniques, crafts, and arts. Since experience is the basis of all science, one can easily see how the many years of experience added to the African frame of mind. Quite clearly, practice is the test of all techniques and all techniques are tried and tested by logic and common sense. Only in the extension of theory, that is, its elaboration, do we have a fuller understanding of how technique and science are similar. In Africa, where humans have existed the longest, science has evolved to address issues such as food, shelter, clothes, and the challenge of fire. These are the most critical activities in human culture.

In Egypt we have the longest written records of African civilization. Therefore it is important that we understand the source of its philosophy. The Nile River is the longest river in the world. It starts almost at the center of Africa and runs down toward the Mediterranean Sea, fanning out into a delta, a distance of 4187 miles (6737 km). The delta is formed by the rich soil left by the river as it empties into the sea. Along this river were some of the earliest human civilizations, communities of people who figured out how to live with each other without killing each other or being killed by their environment. Think of the fact that the longest river and the largest desert are both in Africa and both had an impact on Egypt. The river is the source of life and fertility. It was respected as the deity, Hapi.

One of the ancient hymns of Egypt says, "Hail to you, O Nile, that springs out of the earth and comes to give life to Egypt!"

The Nile gave its abundant gifts to the earliest settlers along its banks. Here on either side of the river were villages and towns that were to give Africa its earliest organized civilization. Towns such as Esna and Edfu stretch back so far into antiquity that their origins remain hidden in the early legends of the valley. Other river valleys and regions on the continent would become important in the years to come, but—it was the Nile, above all other rivers, that was to set the tone for African civilization, that is, how African people would approach ways of living together in peace.

The Nile overflowed its banks every year beginning in June. The people called this the **Inundation.** When the waters reached their peak in September and began to recede the people called the new season the **Emergence.** This period lasted until February, when there would be **Drought** until the waters began to rise at Inundation in June. Each year was the same.

During **Emergence,** the Egyptians trapped water in ponds and human-made lakes to use later for irrigation. They planted seeds in the rich soil left by the river. During **Inundation** the king employed farmers as artisans and builders.

Measurement experts monitored the height of the river. They were the first people to provide detailed information on the rising of flood waters. They could tell by the height of the river upstream how high the flood waters would rise downstream. Therefore, the experts in Aswan (Syene) knew exactly what height the waters would be at a certain date near Abydos and predicted the amount of food that would later be harvested because of the Inundation.

Everything depended on the precision of the experts. If the waters did not rise to a certain level, the farmers would have to carry water from the Nile in buckets to their farms. But think of it, this would be sufficient if you have prepared enough buckets for transporting the water from the river. The Nile flows from the interior of Africa, from the highland areas where there are mountains and hills, down toward the North; Upper Egypt was the South and Lower Egypt was the North. The Nile empties into the Mediterranean Sea in the North.

The great river connected all Egyptians from South to North to one country and in the process created a united community. Hundreds of villages dotted the banks of the river, and traders sailed with ease up and down the length of the country. The Nile River defined the limits of the Egyptian civilization, but it did not define the limits of the imagination of the people.

The ancient African people affectionately called their land **Kemet,** the Land of Blacks, before the Greeks gave it the name of Aegyptos, Egypt. The glyphs for Kemet begin with a piece of charcoal and normally end with a determinative meaning country, nation, town, place, society. The term "The Land of Blacks" did not refer to dirt, as some have assumed, but to the people— black people.

Kemet, like Sudan in Arabic and Ethiopia in Greek, carried a meaning that related to the people themselves. In the case of the Kemetic people, however, they named themselves. Even today, those who travel to Egypt, the ancient Kemet, recognize the presence of African people who look no different from most African Americans. Indeed, the favorite name for African Americans among the Egyptians from Luxor southward is "Nubian Americans." The term Nubian has come to mean those Egyptians who have black skin. Of course, there is a large Arab population in contemporary Egypt and sometimes when people look at Egypt today they are confused by the many complexions of the people. However, it is clear in the minds of most Egyptians and scholars that ancient Egyptians looked more like the present day Nubians than the present day Arabs. Actually, the Nubians are the direct descendants of the people who built the massive stone monuments in the Nile Valley. Furthermore, the ancient Egyptians ranged in complexion and build like present day African Americans, African Brazilians, Ethiopians, or Nigerians. But it is the mind of Africa that is far more significant in this work than the physical complexion of the ancient Egyptians. No one can deny the variety of ideas that have come out of Africa from the beginning of recorded history.

Nevertheless, the fact that the mind of Africa is a composite of all of the rich streams of thought that have enriched the human personality in Africa is proof enough of the diversity and the unity of the ideas that were first presented in written form in the ancient Nile Valley. This diversity is a human trait and the unity is representative of the convergence of African ideals.

CHAPTER TWO: THE FOUR CELESTIAL ELEMENTS

The Essential Questions

What is the meaning of life? What is the source of life? What is the purpose of our lives? Is there a meaning to the universe, to our daily existence, to our life and death? What is the value of human interaction or the value of the divine? It would take the development of cosmogonies to help humans answer these questions.

The emergence of written cosmogonies, the first ordering of human thought, was an Egyptian affair before any other people as far as history now knows. How the world began in the ancient Egyptian mind is a good enough place to begin our discussion of the four celestial elements. The cosmogonies of African philosophers evolved out of religion, as is all philosophy. Religion told them how the world came into being and named the first substances. It was no different in the early days of Egypt's awakening on the continent of Africa.

Egypt was a mighty country, but it had always relied upon the Nile. The struggle to separate the land from the water became, in a profound sense, the most meaningful aspect of the cosmogony of the Egyptian. When it flooded, water was everywhere. They had only to look about them and see that what mattered to humans was the managing of water. Indeed, in the beginning of things, the divine only had to say the equivalent of "Let the dry land appear" and the Egyptian would know that God had spoken. Everything was water, and this was the way the

Egyptians saw it. Whether it was Amen sitting on a hillock separating the water from the land or Ptah standing on the sacred mound, the impact was the same. The idea was that water was the source of all things. Later, the Greeks explained their cosmogony by leaving out the African Amen and Ptah, thus claiming the same ground as the Egyptians but without the divine. Thus, Thales, like the Egyptians, said that everything was once water, but he taught that the earth was formed out of water by a natural process.

The Greeks adapted the Egyptians' original ideas by excluding Amen, Ptah, Atum, and Ra. Thus, they were able to combine many theories of the Egyptians into one coherent whole because they eliminated any contradictory information that may have come out of religious adherences. It was not so much of a *reflection* that brought the Greeks to this place of abstraction as it was the first hint of national jealousy. They could accept the Egyptian explanations but not the Egyptian gods; this is the fact attested to in the early works of Thales, Anaximander, and Anaximenes. Much like a Chinese could learn subjects taught at American universities but remain essentially rooted in Confucian philosophy, the ancient Greeks rarely gave up their religion for that of the Egyptians even though they accepted the wisdom of the Egyptians.

Like Thales, Anaximander was from Miletus, and he is the second important name in European philosophy. He made extensive observations and his observations and reflections were turned toward a study of techniques and the phenomena of nature. Anaximander understood all that he had learned from the Egyptians, and this is why he posited the idea of the four elements as the basis for understanding the world.

The general understanding ran something like this: the earth was at the center with water covering it, mist above the water, and fire embracing all. The fire heating the water caused it to evaporate and it made the dry land appear. This understanding and rendering of the cosmogony of the universe was a condensation of the Egyptian conception of the universe, which included God.

Every philosopher who undertook the study of life and death had to confront the issue of the origin of the universe. Since the origin of the universe had pretty much been established by the time of Imhotep and the Old Kingdom it was not an issue that would trouble the philosophers who came later. For most of them, certainty had been established in the creation and origin of the universe. Things were set, the order had been given, and there was nothing more that humans had to ask of the universe; now all things depended upon how well humans operated within the framework of the universe's own constitution.

It was fairly clear that the object of all inquiries was to show the unshowable or to describe the indescribable in language and terms that would reflect the movement toward Maat, which was understood as the chief end to which all human behavior was geared. One could not do that without some appreciation of the origins of the celestial powers, and indeed, the terrestrial powers as creations of the celestial powers. This was the mystery that would give the name "hidden" to Amen.

What was it that needed to be grasped, explained, or determined if one were to walk the road of Maat? To the philosopher this was simple and needed only a recounting of events to settle the record. One might call this "ethical philosophy" if one were to apply a Western orientation to the questions raised by the ablest African philosophers. However, it is better to view these questions as the basis of all viable human societies where the issues of why are we here and what purpose are we serving constantly agitate the mind of the conscious.

To answer these questions were not thought to be some process of compartmentalization but rather the only real way of assessing why one gets up in the morning to face the new sun. And because these questions were settled in the minds of the ancient Egyptians they had a wonderful approach to the new day. They saw it as the first day toward their new beginning.

They knew that before here and after, light and dark, coming and going, satisfactory and unsatisfactory, yesterday and tomorrow, negative and positive, presence and absence, life and death, there was one comprehensive divinity, an all-encompassing power, alone, unique, distinct, and inherent in the cosmic, watery Nun.

This incomprehensible One in the indefinable cosmic sea was the infinite source of the universe, but itself outside of any concept of time and space. None of the philosophers that I discuss in this book differed in their views. Every seat of instruction and every center of initiation reiterated this concept of the One. Whether the philosopher was a student of Heliopolis, Memphis, Hermopolis, or Thebes (Greek names for On, Men-nefer, Dhuty, Waset, respectively), every major site of the professional priesthood came to the same conclusion about the nature of the One and the creation of the universe.

What differed from time to time was the name of the One who was called Ptah, Ra, Atum, and even Amen or Amen-Ra in later times. Nevertheless, like the names of the Supreme Deity in Yoruba, Akan, Ibo, Christianity, Islam, and Judaism, the functions and roles of the Deity in Kemet remained the same through these various transformations.

The name *ntr* usually rendered in English as "netcher," refers to the divine, divinity, and can be translated as deity or god, yet the ancient Kemetic philosophers understood something more by this term. For them, the ntr (or the plural *ntrw,* rendered "netcheru" in English) was more like the totality of the divine, the all-encompassing universal transgenerational One. While netcheru may be thought of as divinity, that is, the collectivity of the divine, the netcher was the singular expression of divinity. There are some Afrocentrists who are now exploring the relationship of ancient Kemetic language to various forms of expression found in English. Thus, they contend that the English word *nature* may have derived from neter, netcher. I do not know this as a fact from my own investigations but it is a plausible idea and one that must be pursued.

Clearly one cannot discuss African philosophers without a discussion of the creation. Since everything is everything else, the integral nature of the philosophy to the concept of the universe is practically binding on the would-be interpreter. This takes us back to the principles that seem to appear and re-appear throughout the philosophers' works anyway.

How They Saw It

The early Africans believed that the first impulse of the One is to realize consciousness. The neter must realize its own consciousness in order to be divine. Without consciousness there can be no creation because there is no sense that creation is necessary or even possible. It is only through consciousness that the One realizes aloneness, uniqueness, and distinctiveness.

What can best represent this act of origination but the symbol of an arm that draws a bow and is about to let an arrow fly, or a boomerang which is thrown and returns to the thrower after reaching its goal. These are the images that are portrayed in the text to represent the idea of origination, initiation of consciousness.

Actualization is represented in *mdt ntr* as a scarab beetle, Khepri, which passes through the egg, larva, and nymph stages before realizing its winged form. By observation of this relatively common beetle, the ancient Egyptians found the key to the universe as they had come to see it. They believed that the scarab beetle held the secrets to the meaning of transformation, evolution, and even in a political sense, radicalization, if one understood that all change had to do with the discovery of stages and the movement from one stage to another. Indeed Khepri is the act of becoming rather than the process of becoming. Nothing is ever static.

The oldest religious texts are the Pyramid Texts from the tombs of Teti, Unas, and Pepi, the burial chambers of the Fifth and Sixth Dynasties. There, long vertical columns of glyphs engraved on stone walls meant to facilitate the king's ascension into heaven and his return to the side of his father, the incomprehensible One, describe in detail the life and the beliefs of the deceased. Thus, one reads of indestructibility and eternity.

At Heliopolis, the way the story is told is that Atum becomes Khepri, the Scarab Beetle, and in consciousness must project himself or distinguish himself from the Nun as Atum-Khepri.

Atum-Khepri spits out Shu, air; spits out Tefnut, moisture; spits out Geb, earth, and spits out Nut, the sky. These are the four celestial powers. But soon the creation of the terrestrial powers ensues, and Ausar, Auset, Set, and Neb-het are brought into existence. It is written, however, that none are separate from Atum. The Great Ennead is the eight plus Atum, which will order the becoming.

As the Heliopolitans saw it, Atum created the universe by self-coagulation, by his semen or the projection of his heart. The male seed becomes a styptic impulse, a catalyst, which causes the first primordial hill.

As the Memphites saw it, Ptah created the universe by the spoken word. He opened his mouth and spoke and the universe

18

came into being. There is nothing that was created that was not created by Ptah. All creeping things, flying things, and things that grow in the earth were created by Ptah when he sat upon a hillock overlooking the primeval waters and started the creation.

All things that came into being came into being because of the divine One who made them come into being. So it was not just the organic creation that Ptah made, not just the animals, fowls, and fish but also all concepts came into being as aspects of the primordial eight who appeared at Hermolis. They were Naun and Nuanet, Heh and Hehet, Kek and Keket, and Niau and Niaut, and they represented the various aspects of human conceptual existence. This Ogdoad, the eight, are fathers and mothers of Ra, who bring the divine into existence. The child who emerges from the primordial lotus, the principle of light itself, is Ra.

It is often said that Ra is himself the sun. Many texts affirm that Ra penetrates the solar globe and causes it to shine, so that he renders it luminous by his passage. Ra is not light but that which provokes the phenomenon of light, the principle. It might be said that Ra is the most common name for the ancient deity because of the many transformations of Ra. For example, Ra is Atum-Ra at Heliopolis, Ra-Horakhty at Memphis, and Amen-Ra at Thebes. Ra has also been known as Ra-Khepri.

The characteristics of the neter in ancient Kemetic thought are clearly related to the solution of all human problems. In fact, the neter can do this because there is no end to the divine's powers of transformation and transmutation. It is one long litany of achievement. So the neter can say:

> I am One that transforms into two
> I am two that transform into four
> I am four that transforms into Eight
> after this I am ONE.

This is why we say that the African ideal of wholism is reality; it is not simply the wish of intellectuals but the way the masses of people grasped the meanings of the ancients. Their pathways across the deserts, in the Sahel, and in the sanctuaries of the past are testaments to the power of the word as a transformative agent. Only the human can activate the god. One must certainly be careful how the word is spoken because when it is spoken it creates an awesome power. We speak and the words are life, they are material and substantive. It should be in the West as it has been in Africa, and particularly as it was conceived of in the Nile Valley, that one's word is a living word, *ankh medu.*

Such a living word permeates everything when it is spoken with power and honesty. That is why we say that some of our preachers "can really preach." This means that they know how to activate the god. They bring forth the power that was mistakenly called by Westerners "magic." Since all magic is word magic and there is no magic without the word, what they were seeing or experiencing or trying to analyze was the way the African world approached the generative powers of the spoken word.

CHAPTER THREE: IMHOTEP AND THE EMERGENCE OF REASON

The appearance of Imhotep approaches the beginning of human consciousness as written in history. He is before all of the great names in antiquity and stands near the top of the ancients in terms of his display of genius. In Imhotep we have a person who would be important to us if we knew no more than the fact that he was a personality, definite and concrete, in historical time. Being the first such individual recorded means that there is something pristine, pure about him and we are indebted to him and those who lived around his time for the preservation of his knowledge about ancient Africa.

A discussion of Imhotep is critical to an interpretation of the ancient philosophy of the Egyptians since he was the world's first multi-dimensional personality and his achievements stand at the very dawn of reason and science in the service of human society. Furthermore, an examination of Imhotep's beliefs, as interpreted from his life and works, will introduce us to the original thoughts of the first master builder in history.

But how is this to be done since we do not have any major extant documents written by Imhotep at this time? Nothing has been discovered stating in explicit terms what his philosophical ideas were at the time of his greatest activity. Of course, one of the great documents of the Middle Kingdom Period (1991–1786 BC), the so-called Banquet Song, speaks of both Imhotep and the philosopher Hardedef in favorable terms. In fact, the writer says, "I have heard the discourses of Imhotep and Hardedef with whose words men speak everywhere...." So we encounter a popular Imhotep in the writings of others, but we have not discovered his own writings. In this sense, he is rather like Socrates, the Greek, who would live nearly 2,200 years later. What we know of Socrates is from what others wrote about him.

We know factual information about the man Imhotep from various documents, paintings, stelae, and sculptures, most of them from third parties often removed by generations from Imhotep himself. Thus, we are confronted with a unique problem in the history of philosophy, that is, we see evidences of thought, indications of intellectual reflections, as well as read the testimonies of others regarding the brilliance of Imhotep, yet we are left without a written document.

I address this knotty problem by considering ancient Egypt, as it should always be seen, within the context of African history. Nothing emerges so early or palpable as a definite, planned, and reasoned motivation in African history as Imhotep's most remarkable contribution to civilization, the Step Pyramid of Djoser at the Saqqara Cemetery. Of course, this is not his only contribution. We know he was a great physician and was one of the first persons to leave information about the diagnosis of diseases. A mathematical genius, Imhotep invented so many of the earliest instruments of measurement that it is difficult to conceive of the Step Pyramid complex or the stage for the Heb-Sed without him. In dealing with the problems of space and volume in the Step Pyramid, Imhotep not only provided a strategy for explaining what was necessary, he achieved something that had never been accomplished before him.

The Step Pyramid of Saqqara shows reflection, thought, aesthetic sensibilities, balance, harmony, historical insight, reason, and contemporary awareness of the political situation of the time. Any builder would therefore have to have an immense ability to bring disparate ideas together into a coherent whole. One cannot claim to know human history without some appreciation for the accomplishment of Imhotep in the Step Pyramid.

In its conception, construction, and use, the Step Pyramid was a place where the pharaoh and the priest could hold intimate dialogues with the neters in the presence of the people or where the dead could be buried and honored forever. The Step Pyramid Complex, which included courtyards, false temples, underground tunnels, and connecting porticos, was humankind's first statement of the desire for permanence on a grand scale. The preservation of the king's body, like the preservation of the nation itself, was the responsibility of the priests who knew the ancient rules and practices. Imhotep, as one of them, understood the nature of the building profession because to him, as to others, it meant definiteness.

Of course Imhotep was not just a builder, he was a philosopher of the human body and the human mind. In his work he drew upon the natural laws which taught the ancient Kemites so much about the proper flow of life. No other ancient people practiced medicine to the degree and with the perfection of the ancient Kemites. Their medical schools attached to the priesthood and the temples were known for their ability to heal the sufferings of humanity. In fact, Homer attests to this during the 8th century BC when he exclaimed that in medicine "the Egyptians leave the rest of the world behind." However, nearly 2000 years before the arrival of Homer in Egypt, Imhotep had pioneered in the area of medical science. But the ancient Egyptians recognized those who were responsible for healing, such as gods like Ptah, who healed the sick at Memphis before Imhotep, Auset, the great healer of Philae, Khnum, the master healer of Aswan (Syene), or human personalities like Imhotep or Amenhotep, Son of Hapu. They were all highly regarded and venerated.

The Egyptian Philosophers:
Ancient African Voices from Imhotep to Akhenaten

Imhotep appears in history as the vizier of the pharaoh, Djoser, in the Third Dynasty, around 2980–2900 BC. He impressed his colleagues with his great skill at healing and was the first person raised to the status of a demigod for medicine and eventually to the level of a deity. Imhotep was the son of the outstanding architect Kanofer and his wife, Khreduonkh. One of the many attributes of Imhotep was that he was well trained and educated in all of the sciences and arts of ancient Egypt. He was erudite, studious, well read in the traditions, and given to a liberal understanding of science. As a philosopher Imhotep was equipped for his role as the first major thinker in human history. His titles included Grand Vizier, Architect, Physician, Chief Lector Priest or Kheri-heb, Astronomer, Scribe, Orator usually called Magician by European scholars, and Philosopher. No other human prior to Imhotep had ever claimed so many titles of intellect, eloquence, and science.

As vizier, Imhotep was the King's Prime Minister. He was responsible for the daily running of the administration of the country, including jurisdiction over the King's records, criminal and civil cases, bearer of the royal seal, chief of all public works, and supervisor of everything in the entire land. This meant he was responsible for the treasury, war, the judiciary, interior, agriculture, and the executive. In holding the office of vizier and confidante to an important king, Imhotep set the tradition which would be followed by two other great philosophers, Ptahhotep and Amenhotep, son of Hapu.

The legend of the Seven Years' Famine has established Imhotep's reputation as a man of wisdom. This was a period of great famine and terrible starvation all over Egypt caused by the failure of the Nile River to reach its usual flood level for seven years in a row. The result was catastrophic on the agricultural sector. Some thought that the lack of water was due to the fact that the king had neglected to pay homage, honor, and worship to the god Khnum, the deity who controlled the river from Elephantine Island.

In this moment of crisis, Djoser turned to his chief counselor and advisor, Imhotep, for advice. He inquired about the origin of the Nile and the deity who ruled at the source of the river. Imhotep demonstrated an intense sense of science and research when he indicated that he could not answer the king before consulting the sacred books for an answer. This is history's first recorded example of a person searching ancient books, books more ancient than his own time, for answers to a contemporary problem. Two aspects of Imhotep's intelligence are revealed in his response to the king. In the first place, he did not think that he knew everything. In the second place he knew that it was necessary to consult the books, the more ancient books. In the first instance Imhotep, with all of his brilliance and despite the high regard with which he was held in the royal court, knew that he did not have all the answers. This demonstrates that his ego was under control.

He also placed confidence in the work of others, which is why he consulted the books. When Imhotep had completed his investigation he reported to the king the hidden things which had not been shown to a king for unimaginable ages. On hearing the report of Imhotep the king wrote to Meter, the King of Nubia, asking for his assistance in abating the terrible state of affairs. He wanted Meter to give him advice about which deity to approach in order that the granaries of Egypt would be refilled. In time, Djoser went to Elephantine to visit the temple of Khnum to make prayers and supplications before him. Soon thereafter, Khnum appeared before the king in a dream and promised that the Nile should rise and never fail again. He was told that plants shall bend beneath their produce, want shall cease, and the emptiness of the granaries shall come to an end. Because of Khnum's intervention the king gave the temple of Khnum lands and gifts of gold, ivory, ebony, spices, woods, and precious stones.

Imhotep was the chief of all the works of the king and in this capacity was the builder of the Saqqara Pyramid, known as the Step Pyramid. This pyramid is thought of as a transition from the mastaba type tomb to the true pyramid. It is, however, evidence of the creative ingenuity of Imhotep the architect, that he was able to build upon the mastaba idea and pave the way for the true pyramid type. The Step Pyramid is the earliest tomb construction of such massive size known to humans. To build such a major tomb meant that the kingdom must have had enough wealth to achieve the building, along with a stable government, skilled workers, ability to keep complex records, and a means of transporting the large stones.

Imhotep is associated with the early temple at Edfu. Completed in 57 BC, this temple's inscription mentions Imhotep as a great priest who lectures. Perhaps in his capacity as an architect who lectures we get some idea of Imhotep as a Kheri-heb, a Chief Lector Priest, a professor. This is the priest who is allowed to read from the sacred books and to recite the holy words of the gods. Since according to the Egyptian belief these texts had magical powers, the Kheri-heb was seen also as a magician.

Taking part in ceremonies such as the liturgy of funerary offerings, the Kheri-heb would recite the formulas while the Sem priest officiated most of the rituals. When the Kheri-heb recited the sacred formula during the presentation of gifts to the dead, the formula was to change the food or gift into something divine and spiritual. This was then partaken by the soul of the departed. In the Opening of the Mouth ceremony, the idea was to restore to the corpse the abilities it had enjoyed during life. The mouth was symbolically opened so that the mummy might speak and the eyes touched so that the eyes might see. Here the Kheri-heb was in charge and was assisted by the Sem priest. Clearly, the Kheri-heb was held in highest esteem throughout the country. In fact, the Egyptian people believed that the Kheri-heb mediated between the King and the deities.

Although Imhotep held his role as the Kheri-heb in high regard and was evidently very good at it, he was known best for his work in medicine. The two roles, that of Kheri-heb, which included magic, and that of physician were often merged in the career of this mighty personality. It was his excellent skills as a physician that led to his deification. Imhotep healed many people and created some of the cures that became standard in Egypt and the world. Imhotep was the first historical person to be made a god. Less than fifty years after his death, King Menkaure made a temple for him, thus officially deifying Imhotep.

The manner Imhotep went about his healing work is instructive in attempting to understand the early days of medicine. Many of the papyri on magic are filled with medical prescriptions. The medical papyrus, Ebers, is full of incantations. In establishing the tradition of incantations with healing disease, Imhotep set the stage for the whole of African medicine in which the physician always accompanies the healing process with incantations. The philosophy was that the medicine could not heal unless it had been made powerful by the energy that came with the spoken word. Unquestionably, Imhotep was the most significant multi-genius of his age and the first human to combine so many talents into one personality. His medical achievements created the aura that still surrounds his name and his fame is eternal.

As a philosopher and scribe, Imhotep demonstrated he was multi-talented. Perhaps it was his intelligence, practicality, and high office that led to his eminent success as a physician. One could certainly see how people would be inclined to believe in the medicine of such an individual. His credibility only increased with the Egyptians' knowledge of his many gifts. He held the reputation in Egypt as one of the greatest of Egyptian philosophers and the earliest of physicians and his fame for wisdom and medicine made such an impression on his fellow Egyptians that it endured as a national tradition for years.

Imhotep's medical, philosophical, and architectural works were extant even in the early days of the Christian era. Indeed, he was worshipped well into the fifth century AD. He wrote on some general topics as well as the specific scientific issues of medicine, architecture, and astronomy. According to one account, his proverbs were handed down from generation to generation and were noted for their grace and diction. He was called "The Patron of Scribes" because of beautiful poetry. A song known as the "Song of the Harper" includes his name. It was a favorite of the Egyptians because it contained the philosophy of "eat and drink because tomorrow we die." One can compare this with the scripture in I Corinthians 15:32. The oldest version of this poem appears on the tomb of the Theban King Antef.

> All hail to the prince, the good man,
> whose body must pass away,
> while his children remain here.
> The gods of old rest in their tombs,
> And the mummies of men long dead;
> The same for both rich and poor.
> The words of Imhotep, I hear.
> The words of Hardedef, which say:
> What is prosperity? Tell!
> Their fences and walls are destroyed,

Their houses exist no more;
And no man comes again from the tomb
To tell what passes below.
You go to the place of the mourners,
To the grave whence none return;
Strengthen your hearts to forget your joys,
Yet fulfil our desires while you live.
Anoint yourselves, clothe yourselves well,
Use the gifts which the gods bestow,
Fulfil your desires upon earth.
For the day will come to you all
When you hear not the voices of friends
When weeping avails you do more.
So feast in tranquility now.

One cannot judge Imhotep's philosophy from such a small representative of his thought. But obviously he was a man who produced a considerable corpus during his lifetime. His reputation is enduring precisely because he engaged the major issues of morality, health, science, and ethics.

King Menkaure, the son of Khufu, for whom one of the great pyramids of Giza was erected, was the first king to build a temple for Imhotep, according to one of the Oxyrhynchus Papyri, written in Greek and dating from the second century AD. Thus, we see that Imhotep was worshipped as early as the fourth dynasty and his temple was a place frequented by the sick and afflicted.

Nechautis, the author of the Oxyrhynchus Papyrus about Imhotep, developed his story from the ancient records found in Imhotep's temple. Nechautis wanted to prove that he was the proper person to hold the title of priest of Imhotep and that he had the authority to pass the title to his posterity.

To honor Imhotep, Nechautis resolved to translate into Greek an ancient Egyptian book; it is not clear if this was written by Imhotep or not, but I presume it was. He complained that he did not think he was old enough to complete the task properly or to do justice to the god Imhotep and that he feared his inability. The Greek name for Imhotep was Aesclapius found in the Hippocratic oath.

Actually the story is told that Nechautis' mother was stricken with malarial fever and was so ill that her friends assisted her in seeking help from the temple of Imhotep where she was cured with simple remedies. Nechautis and his mother were so impressed and thankful that they made sacrifices and gave gifts to the god Imhotep.

Soon thereafter Nechautis himself became ill with the same violent fever, pain in his side, and a hacking cough. As his mother had done he hastened to the shrine, fell on the floor and immediately lapsed into semi-consciousness. His mother, while wide awake, was visited by a vision of a person of superhuman stature dressed in glistening garments and with a book in his hand. This man examined the patient from head to foot, then quickly faded. When the mother had recovered from the shock of this vision she discovered that her son had lost his fever, he was no longer coughing, and his pain had vanished. The only evidence of his illness was that he was perspiring quite profusely. When the patient could speak he recounted the same vision that the mother had seen while awake.

Again the mother and son expressed their gratitude by the customary donation to the temple. Imhotep was not satisfied and notified Nechautis through a vision that what he required was for Nechautis to complete the promise that he had made earlier to edit and translate the ancient Egyptian book into the Greek language.

Nechautis set about his task and described it in words similar to these:

> *Once you had noticed, divine Master, that I had ne-*
> *glected the divine book filled with your divinity and*
> *invoking your providence, I hastened to the task of*
> *the history. I hope to extend the fame of your creativ-*
> *ity by my proclamation, for I discovered truly by a*
> *physical treatise in another book the account of the*
> *creation of the world. Throughout I have filled up*
> *defects and struck out superfluities....Hence, Master,*
> *I conjecture the book has been completed in accor-*
> *dance with your wishes,...suiting your divinity. As the*
> *discoverer of this art, Aesculapius (Imhotep), greatest*
> *of Gods and my teacher, you are distinguished among*
> *all men. For every gift made with a vow or every sacri-*
> *fice presently perishes, but a written record is an un-*
> *dying reward of gratitude, renewing its youth to the*
> *memory. Every Greek tongue will tell the story and*
> *every man will worship you, Imhotep, the son of Ptah.*

Of course it was in the 18th Dynasty that the custom of the scribes pouring libation to Imhotep was first recorded and the fact that this was so suggests that he was well on his way to god status long before the Persians came in 525 BC, the date normally given for the full divinity of Imhotep. When Cambyses conquered Egypt, Imhotep had made his apotheosis. He was assigned a divine father, Ptah, and became one of the three reigning gods of the sacred city of Memphis: Ptah, Sekhmet, and Imhotep. Worshipped in Egypt, Nubia, and Greece, Imhotep remains one of the greatest in human history.

Indeed during the period of Imhotep's life, medicine was seen as an intellectual challenge. All things that required reflection were philosophical; medicine was therefore a part of the challenge of philosophy. Why did humans get sick? What was the source of affliction? How should one treat the ill? What is the origin of disease itself? These were not merely rhetorical questions for Imhotep, they were real issues that had to be confronted. Many of the works that Imhotep produced are not extant, but it is believed that his medical treatises survived until the Christian era, meaning that they lasted more than 2500 years!

There was a custom that went along with the harper's song that seems strange to us now, but was meaningful to the Egyptians in the days of Imhotep. It was associated with festivities. While people were eating, a man with a harp would carry a wooden corpse among the diners in order to remind them in song and poetry that they should eat and enjoy themselves because soon they would be like the corpse. Imhotep spent his life working in the interest of his state, passing judgments, building monuments, erecting pyramids, writing poetry, healing the sick, and developing the principles of architecture. It was as if he felt that life was too brief to get every thing that he wanted to do into the time that he was allotted.

Yet he bequeathed to posterity a tremendous legacy of work. His reputation brought his deification and there were temples dedicated to him as well as rituals in temples not necessarily associated with him. We know that the temple of Deir-el-Bahari had a chamber built by the Ptolemaic rulers dedicated to Imhotep and Amenhotep, son of Hapu. The idea behind the Greeks' recognition of these two philosophers must have been the attempt to capitalize on their popularity among the masses of people. On the wall of the chamber at Deir-el-Bahari, there is a scene that shows Imhotep carrying a sceptre in one hand and an ankh in the other. The inscription reads, "I have given you life combined with health and protection. I am the protector." Thus, in his capacity as god, Imhotep pronounces his gift.

He was also worshipped at the temple of Ptah at Waset. Built by Tuthmoses III, Imhotep, as the son of Ptah, was revered alongside the black image of Sekhmet, the wife of Ptah, and Amenhotep, son of Hapu. There were many shrines in which Amenhotep and Imhotep, the two most famous philosophers, were worshipped together.

Many festivals were created in Imhotep's honor. Pilgrimages and banquets, music and dance were all part of the celebration of the life of this great man, deified. People would come to express their gratitude for his healing powers and to receive his blessings.

On a statue found in Upper Egypt there is an inscription that begins with an address from Pedi-Bast, a scribe, to Imhotep. It says, "I am your son, perfect in the service of your Ka on all your festival days and the commencement of the seasons and on every festival." There is a discussion of six festivals:

First Festival—May 31
The birthdate of Imhotep.

Second Festival—December 27
The day Sekhmet, beloved of Ptah, ordains and glorifies the image of Imhotep.

Third Festival—June 23
The day of the slaying of the vile Asiatics by Sekhmet. She tears off their limbs and capsizes their boat in the Red Lake.

Fourth Festival—July 1
The day of the lamentations for the death of Imhotep.

Fifth Festival—July 7
The day on which Imhotep reposes before his father after his
death.

Sixth Festival—April 19
The day on which the spirit of Imhotep departs towards the great
place of sojourn in the whole earth.

There can be no question that Imhotep was a special spirit
upon the earth. Many teachers and philosophers who were to
come after him, such as Confucius, Buddha, Jesus, and
Muhammad, gave the world similar reasons to deify them.
Centuries before the Jews, the Greeks, and the Indians,
and long before the birth of Hippocrates, there was in Egypt a
physician so famous for his knowledge and skill in healing disease that he became recognized as the god of medicine. He holds
the greatest place in our hagiology, and though his temple at
Memphis is silent today, he reigns supreme in the hearts of those
who recall his deeds from the old books.

Imhotep

Ptahhotep

CHAPTER FOUR: PTAHHOTEP AND THE MORAL ORDER

The ancient African philosophers understood that the essence of who we are is connected to healthy souls. They believed in the direct relationship of soul and body. How to get the soul to be healthy, therefore, is the principal quest of the writings of someone like Ptahhotep. He is a moral compass, a thermometer, a Nilometer, if you please, seeking to help us determine just how high we are willing to rise to advance ourselves and others. His aim, like that of most of the Egyptian philosophers, was to re-establish the First Occasion in the mind of the people.

In the mind of the Egyptians the deities had already established the path of good and evil and it was up to the living humans to carry out the first occasion.

Isaac Meyer's **Oldest Books in the World** was one of the first books to bring to the attention of the Western world the significance of the philosophers Ptahhotep and the instructions to Kagemni, two ancient Egyptian works included in Meyer's volume. In fact, long before George G.M. James' famous **Stolen Legacy,** Isaac Meyer argued that later Greek philosophy was nothing more than the extension of Egyptian philosophy. Of course, those European writers who have often attacked George G.M. James have simply ignored the white writer Meyer.

Meyer's use of the Papyrus Prisse text for his book suggests that he was convinced of its authenticity. A complete copy of the text is in Papyrus Prisse which is held by the Bibliothèque

Nacionale (National Library of Paris). All translations of the original are derived from the Papyrus Prisse which dates from the Middle Kingdom. Two incomplete copies of the philosophy are found at the British Museum and they are from the Middle and New Kingdoms, respectively. The Carnavon Wooden tablet is held by the Cairo Museum and is dated to the New Kingdom. Like other scholars of Egypt, Meyer had been sufficiently impressed by the Prisse Papyrus, as it was called, to include it as one of the oldest books in the world. When Phillipe Virey published his essay in 1887 on the Prisse Papyrus, he introduced it to the West by providing a transcription of the hieratic text, the graphic Mdu Ntr, a translation into French, and an index.

The critical history of the Prisse Papyrus, which contains the Teaching of Ptahhotep and the work dedicated to Kagemni, has been traced to a commentary by Francois Chabas in 1858. According to Chabas, E. Prisse d'Avenues gave this papyrus to the Bibliotheque Nacionale in Paris and it was subsequently published in 1847. D'Avenues himself had acquired the papyrus from an African he had employed to help excavate the areas at Drah-abu'l-Neqqah, near Thebes. It is thought that the papyrus came from the tomb of Intef I or Intef II and that it speaks to an earlier rather than a later date of origin.

E. A. Wallis Budge translated the Teachings of Ptahhotep in a 1924 book where he also published an account of Kagemni's moral teaching. Budge, a keeper of the Assyrian and Egyptian Antiquities at the British Museum, wrote prodigiously on various aspects of the Egyptian culture. While his translations have been superseded by more expert renderings, his work remains extensive and instructive. The older writers such as Meyers and Budge have contributed to our understanding, although their works have been questioned by more expert analysis.

Of all the earlier Egyptian philosophers, Ptahhotep best represents the traditions of the moral order. He was a late Fifth Dynasty (2414– 2375 BCE) philosopher whose work provides a comprehensive discussion of ethical behavior and moral philosophy.

The Early Philosophical Writings were sometimes called Instructions by the ancient Egyptians, but the term carried a far more substantive meaning than the English "directions." To the ancient Egyptians, the thoughts and ideas of the wise were instructive for the pursuit of *Maat*. In fact, in an attempt to deal with this differentiation, Western Egyptologists called these writings "Instructions in Wisdom" or "Wisdom Literature." The word "philosophia" itself in the Greek language meant "friend of wisdom." I have chosen to call them what they best represent, "Early Philosophical Writings," or I have used the Egyptian term "seboyet" to describe the works. In the Mdu Ntr, the word carries a star sign as one of its glyphs indicating perception, insight, and light, i.e., wisdom.

It is significant that Ptahhotep was the first person to address good manners and style. The name Ptahhotep means "Ptah is satisfied" or "Peace belongs to Ptah." The entire title of the treatise reads "Precepts of the Perfect, the Feudal Lord, Ptahhotep, under the Majesty of the King of the South and of the North, Assa, Living Eternally, Forever." Everything that we know about Ptahhotep suggests that he would favor good manners, propriety, peace, and justice over chaos and disorder. By his name we know that he is dedicated to the Almighty God.

Furthermore, Ptahhotep claims to be one hundred and ten years old, a figure frequently found in the ancient Kemetic literature. As such he is one very capable of giving advice in the African sense because he had attained a good old age. Wisdom itself comes from the experiences of age and Ptahhotep had lived long enough to pass knowledge on to children. But there is something else here and that is the fact that Ptahhotep is the son of the king. He is of royal blood and therefore his words reflect studied answers to the questions of life. Leisure time, the ancients believed, was the source of much reflection. Ptahhotep appears to have had a considerable amount of time for reflection.

With the glory of his age wrapped around his heart and out of the boundless joy of his wisdom, Ptahhotep probably retired from the position of influence that he held from the time of his youth to give advice to his son, indeed, to all human beings. In one sense, his philosophy is addressed to his son but in a larger sense, as we shall see, he addresses humanity. There is so much that an elder can teach if he or she has been attuned to the manifest ways in which humans conquer evil and death. What Ptahhotep concludes is that the Deity would not allow him, even in his old age, to become useless.

Thus, because he is old and his son young, Ptahhotep addresses his philosophy to his son, who was expected to become, as his father was, an officer in the kingdom. Consequently the words written by Ptahhotep are the result of reflection, reason, and a desire to explain to his son the most perfect path to the best life and immortality.

His work is essentially 37 maxims that have come down to us in the form of ethical instructions. The work survived from the Old Kingdom period in four copies, three written on papyrus and one containing only the first part written on a wooden tablet. Obviously, the philosophy of Ptahhotep was considered by the Egyptians to be of great value and certainly worth preservation. Thus, although the original text was written in the Old Kingdom period, the extant copies available to us are from the Middle or

New Kingdom. Nevertheless, we have enough of Ptahhotep's thinking in the text to know that he was a person of deep contemplation.

An overwhelmingly African sensibility seems to infuse the maxims that are given by Ptahhotep. One is reminded of the proverbs of the Igbo or Asante people when one reads the maxims of Ptahhotep; the similarity resides in the intense humanism of the maxims. He is concerned with issues of moderation, generosity, kindness, respect, integrity, justice, and self-control. One fails to find any of the virtues of a martial society, such as valor, courage, bravery, or even prowess, as one would find in some other ancient societies. There is no hint of ill-will here, no glorying in war where one slaughters the enemies and scatters them to the wind. There is no grand boasting of the prowess of the warrior or the cleverness of the aggressor; there is only what is right and what is in the interest of harmony in the community.

Cynthia Lehman (1997) has shown in a survey of general values and themes among Middle Kingdom philosophers that the following were most common: respect for proper speech, respect for elders and leaders, ritual remembrance, good behavior, absence of arrogance, lack of threats, absence of gossip, submission to authority, pursuit of truth, attainment of justice, generosity, self-control, impartiality, avoidance of hasty speech, masking one's inner feelings, and good listening skills. This is not to say that other virtues did not exist in the society but rather that they must not have ranked as high as the ethical principles articulated by Ptahhotep. In his mind, as has been shown in more recent African philosophy, relationships carried more weight in the scale of morality than any other aspect of life. The reason for this is that the collectivity is always stronger than the individual and there should be nothing in our personal cases that would prevent us from seeking the ultimate good of the community. We are the sum total of our relationships.

Ptahhotep reflects on old age itself in this passage:

"O king, my lord
I am old, old age has finally arrived
I was first feeble, but now I am weak also
Like a child I sleep all day
And when I wake, my eyes are dim and my
    ears deaf
My strength wanes with weariness
My tongue is silent
My memory is dead
And arthritis wreaks havoc on my bones
Sweetness becomes bitterness, my taste is gone
Surely old age affects everything
The sinuses are clogged
And it is painful to stand or to sit.
(Translation by author)

Here in a prologue to instruction, Ptahhotep lays out frankly the condition of aging. This is the first record in history of anyone stating so clearly how the body is affected by the ravages of time. One can see that the author is setting the stage for his lessons, but finds it necessary to establish the authority that has been vested in him because of his age. You can imagine what the age of 110 meant in Ptahhotep's day, whether it was an illusionary or real date. To say that you are that old even now means that those who are younger know that you have something profound to contribute.

A friend of mine, John Burton of Philadelphia, went with me to Egypt in 1998 when he was 80. I shall never forget the two hour conversation about age I had with him sailing up the Nile River. He told me that he wanted to study for seven more years and then at 87 review what he had studied for the previous forty two years until he was a hundred. "But what have you learned?" I asked him. "What do you think you still have to learn?" To understand my questions to him you must know that in Philadelphia he was a retired municipal employee who had made an avocation out of etymology and he knew the meanings and origins of hundreds of words in the English language. He said to me, "I have learned that I do not know as much as I thought I did when I was 70 and I still have to learn how the ancient Egyptian philosophers confronted the problem of not knowing." The "Professor," as he is affectionately known to the hundreds of students he has instructed in etymology, had just indicated that the ancient Egyptians were the barometer to him that they were to me. He knew that I loved to read Ptahhotep and he posed a situation that I could not answer. I could only wonder what the philosophers did with the problem of not knowing. Nevertheless, I believe that Ptahhotep realized that it was necessary to have humility in the face of the unknown because he wanted in his son the characteristics that would make him successful. This is the beginning of a pedagogy of morality.

What is more, Ptahhotep establishes some of the principal themes of the ancient African educational process, namely, respect for age and respect for leadership. The ancient Egyptians knew that it was necessary in any case for the people of a country to accept the moral and experienced leadership of the nation, otherwise there would be difficulty and confusion. Ptahhotep places the issue of age squarely before his son in terms of authority and it echoes to us in this generation.

Listen as Ptahhotep continues his prologue in this manner:

> May old age serves me as a staff
> So that I may repeat the words of those who
> heard
> The words of the ancestors
> Who listened to the gods.
> I want the same thing done for you
> So that strife may disappear from among the
> people
> And the people of both banks of the river serve
> you!
> The majestic God said, therefore,
> Instruct him in the words of the past
> That he become a model for posterity
> May he be obedient
> May he be devoted to the one who speaks to
> him
> Because no one is born with wisdom.
> (Translation is author's.)

Ptahhotep knew that Egyptians believed that age was an authority, a staff for speaking the words of the ancestors who were closest to the gods. In a sense, the young man who would receive the instructions, the wisdom, the philosophy, would be receiving the fundamental ethical principles that had governed the ancestors. The young man should become a model for the children of the great who would come after him, but this was impossible unless he was obedient and devoted to the words of the wise. No one, of course, is born wise.

There is, of course, in Ptahhotep the incredible allegiance to the African idea of stability, *djed,* as it applied to human relationships as well as to the structures of society. Egyptians were impressed by continuity, and they were determined to uphold the universe by maintaining Maat.

Ptahhotep sets the path toward his philosophy very soon after his discourse on aging. He asks, Who will give him authority to speak? The answer—the Majestic Deity, who said that he should instruct his son with the words of the former times. This is a major theme in ancient African works. Ptahhotep raises the question of continuity and stability and finds his answer in the way Africans approach information. Ptahhotep seeks to speak the words of those who have spoken before because they are the ones who are closer to the gods.

The Principal Precepts:
1. Do not be arrogant because you know more than others. Perfection in philosophy and in artistry is elusive.

Clearly this is a useful instruction since it is ageless. I will never forget the lesson I learned when I was thirteen. Although I was asked by my teacher to write letters for some of the veterans of Korea, I was also told not to get "a big head," meaning that my writing ability was one of many that humans had been granted and we cannot take credit for the gifts that are ours at birth. All intelligence is a gift from nature and it is foolishness for a person to be arrogant because of knowledge. We are all on the path to perfection.

2. Keep your temper during disputes, and when others lose theirs, be cool.

It is so easy to become agitated when in a dispute, but it is better if you can keep your temper and provide a deliberate and easy-to-follow argument. Anger often prevents clear thinking. So we are cautioned that when others lose their tempers we should retain ours.

This prescription is as effective today as it has been through the ages. When others are in hot temper, angry and upset, then you must be cool and peaceful. In fact, a cool temper is like a breeze in the midst of a suffocatingly humid room. Not long ago one of my colleagues, Abu Abarry, the director of the Temple University Ghana Study Program, told me of how he had to deal with a situation in the dormitory at the University of Ghana. One of his American students was playing music so loud at night that the Ghanaian students complained. The American student then accused the Ghanaians of getting up at 5 AM and making noises, talking and walking the floors, waking others who were trying to sleep. When Abu came upon them they were almost at blows, but his demeanor was so compellingly cool that he was able to resolve the dispute in no time. Apologies were made all around. The music lowered, which left the American with dignity and restored the Ghanaians' sense of pride. Had he been angry with either party, the entire situation would have gotten out of hand. It was Ptahhotep's maxim appearing in a contemporary situation.

3. Do not despise someone because their opinion is different from yours.

Difference in opinions has never harmed anyone; it will not harm anyone. What is sometimes difficult for us to accept is the fact that others may have better opinions than we do. We should learn to cherish the ideas of others as we listen. Imagine how their minds work and seek to affirm them in their diversity. You are not the only one who has ideas, can think, or who is capable of intelligence. Assuming that your ability is unique is a mistake of fools.

4. Justice is great, unchangeable, and certain. The judge should administer it so that peace shall reign.

Fairness helps everyone. Participation in the administration of justice is to be praised, but judges must be just for peace to rule. The great earthly keepers of Maat were the judges who were priests.

5. There is no reason to cause yourself to be feared by others.

Do not encourage either your friends or yourself to be a bully.

The person who is feared by others cannot be trusted. Indeed, the fear of the audience or community often causes individuals to overreact to some nuisances in their lives.

6. Behave well while eating at the home of another.

Good home training will lead to good behavior. One should never enter the home of another and bring attention to one's presence in a negative way. During meals, the visitor must always defer to the hosts.

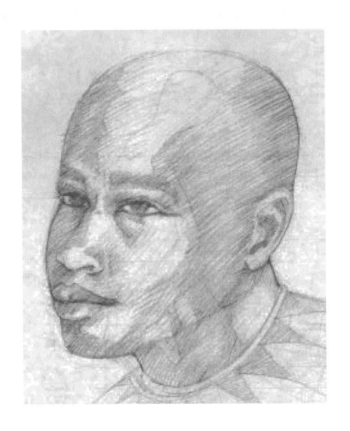

Kagemni

CHAPTER FIVE: INSTRUCTIONS TO KAGEMNI FOR SUCCESS

On a hot summer day one August I visited the tomb of Kagemni in the vicinity of the tomb of Meriruka and the pyramids of Teti and Pepi on the Saqqara plains. Once you pass through the antechamber in the tomb you are confronted with a three-pillared room with reliefs depicting scenes from the life of Kagemni. One gets the sense that he was a man with a passion for life and that he understood the interrelationship of ecology, environment, and human relationships. All of this is depicted in the multi-faceted scenes that adorn the walls of his tomb.

This appreciation of creation and nature was illustrated by the way the artists interpreted Kagemni's career. Among the scenes in the tomb are those of men fishing, crocodiles, dragonflies, grasshoppers, and frogs. Geese are shown in the same scene as hyenas. On a different wall one sees a cow and a small dog. The room to the right of the three-pillared room has several reliefs of animals as well. There are reliefs of greyhounds, monkeys, ducks, geese, and birds. From the richness of this mastaba type tomb one can imagine the importance of a person like Kagemni. He was truly remarkable in his day, and his name has remained with us until now. However, few are familiar with his moral ideas and his ethical principles. What were the key elements in Kagemni's texts?

The remains of Kagemni's text are from a single manuscript which shows a similarity to the work of Ptahhotep. Some scholars have argued that Kagemni's text may have been written by one Kaires who appears in a list of literary figures in the Papyrus Chester Beatty IV, where he is coupled with Ptahhotep on a Saqqara tomb wall. I have followed the more popular line taken by Maulana Karenga that the text of Kagemni reflects the wisdom of a man who was comprehensive in knowledge, broad in interests, and active in the pursuit of natural life. Yet, I have accepted the fact that the instructions appear to be directed toward Kagemni. This does not dilute the idea of Kagemni as a person of considerable means and power.

Kagemni's mastaba is of the Sixth Dynasty. He was a judge, philosopher, and a priest and served as the officer of Snefru and may have served during the reign of Huni as well. In Kemet, the great king almost always had a great prime minister, and no officer was greater for his king than Kagemni. Holding close to his chest the secrets of the king and recognizing Snefru's popularity were partly dependent upon him, Kagemni was steeped in the traditions and philosophies of Kemet. The instructions given to him add to a tradition remarkably well-suited to enrich the philosophical legacy of the ancient Egyptian people.

The text writer wrote about social behavior and the proper conduct toward leaders and fellow human beings. The sage that instructed Kagemni was almost a "house" philosopher, one committed to the idea that the masses must be taught how to respect authority. The text of his work is recorded in the Prisse Papyrus.

One text attributed to Kagemni says:

He who is the priest of the living, whom a god favors like the Bennu bird on the Tekenu performs right actions without seeking a reward for them but sets his heart only on the god's service. He has compassion upon all living creatures. He holds fast to the god's name and inspires others to meditate on it. He accepts joy and sorrow with equanimity. He is always happy and never set apart from his god. To him gold and dross are as one. Nectar and poison are as one. The king and the beggar are as one.

An explanation of this text reveals that the unknown philosopher's renown rested not so much on his statecraft, which evidently was well thought of, but more on his intelligent approach to service and generosity. He proffered a way of looking at the world that involved the true understanding and appreciation of other people and all creatures. He may have been the first ecologically interested philosopher because he spoke on behalf of the principles that demonstrate generosity to the land as well as to the people. To use the Bennu bird, often called the phoenix, and the tekenu or obelisk as figures in his moral teaching also shows a person who is attuned to the myths, intellectual properties, and metaphors of his own time.

A profound attitude toward the earth and a collegiality with other inhabitants of the land were the calling cards of Kagemni's teacher. His way of looking at the world may be contained in what I have called the "six djeds or pillars of Kagemni." They are: devotion, compassion, loyalty, balance, solidarity, and judgment. Let us examine the strengths and lessons inherent in the Papyrus Prisse.

The Six Djeds
Devotion: Kagemni's teacher says that the priest of the living performs right actions without seeking rewards. This is surely a search for the ideal. The philosopher sees the ideal in the priest of the living, i.e., those priests who are engaged in the mediations, and worldly matters involving the living. The priests

51

who officiate for the dead have other responsibilities. But those who minister to the living must have the character to do right without looking for any type of reward; one should do right because it is right. This is the full meaning of devotion. When we think of a full measure of devotion we immediately think of one who is willing to give his or her life for what they believe is right. One can be devoted to another or to a cause, but the highest reward is to be devoted to a cause that involves human beings. The Christians say that Jesus was devoted to sinners because he was willing to give his life that sinners might be saved. Africans point to the sacrifice of Nat Turner, Denmark Vesey, and Gabriel Prosser in the quest for African liberation from enslavement in America. They knew that if they failed in their devotion to their cause they would be killed and yet they continued with their plans.

Compassion: Notice how the philosopher says that the ideal person has compassion for all living creatures. He is suggesting that the ideal person recognizes something in all living creatures that are special, unique, and inherently wonderful. In this respect, the Kagemni instructions helped to mold the Egyptian way of life and the response to the environment. At such an early age in Egyptian history, a philosopher, one given to living, learning, and teaching at the highest levels of his society, was capable of expressing what evidently was already a major aspect of African philosophy, African pacifism, by the 6th Dynasty. All living creatures were worthy of respect and hence compassion. How could a person just cut down a tree, or catch a fish, or kill a goose, or disturb the river without awe at the beautiful harmony in the universe? The teacher of Kagemni was a significant force in cultivating the more compassionate aspects of Kemetic life. One should understand this type of compassion as sympathy with action.

Different families held to various beliefs about the nature of the earth and its bounty. Some people did not kill rams, others did not kill geese, and still others revered the crocodile. Herein is an indication that totemic responses to the environment might be possible and indeed necessary as a way to control human treatment of other living creatures. If one is respectful of all living creatures, one is at heart applying a system of ecological dignity to the animal kingdom that constitutes the ideal. Early on the Africans discovered that wholesale destruction of the environment and abuse to the ecological balance were dangerous to the human community.

Loyalty: Kagemni's teacher holds fast the god's name and teaches others to meditate on it. There is a sense of focus and concentration in the philosopher's understanding of the way one holds fast to the name of the god. He is not simply speaking the name of the god as a mnemonic device, but actually in the way one respects the god's name.

Certain striking advances are noted in the work of this philosopher who may be called one of the earliest Egyptian humanists in the sense that he was an advocate of man, a believer in the possibilities of humans working out government or social relations on the basis of right actions. We have no guarantee of a civilized culture without the idea that a person's word can count for something. Loyalty is based always on trust; credibility depends upon right actions. The author's insistence on holding fast to the god's name is more than a technique to secure an empty allegiance, it is a sincere belief in the idea that if a person is focused, committed to an idea, to a purpose, he or she will excel at all things. This is why we see him as a philosopher of rites, special protocols, and manners; one who is ultimately capable of teaching us about the perfectibility of man.

Balance: Life is fraught with many problems that are capable of creating disequilibrium. Thus, it is necessary for us to have a balanced attitude toward the various situations in which we find ourselves. One must treat with equanimity both sorrow and joy. Some days we will experience more sorrow than joy. On other days our joy will be unending, but in either case we must be prepared to accept both. For the philosopher, this was a form of wisdom. It is foolish to run after pleasure without taking into consideration that pain is also a part of human existence. But it is also vain to wallow in pain as if there is no pleasure. Both are realities of life. Along with the valleys of life, there will always be mountains on the other side.

Solidarity: The statement that the person whom he favors "is always happy and never set apart from his god" could be seen as an expression of solidarity with that which is preeminent. But for one to arrive at such a position of attachment, it is fundamental that knowledge precedes attachment. The philosopher suggests that the votarist is "always happy" and one can argue that the meaning here is that attachment to the god, that is, solidarity with that which is perfection, is the source of happiness. But how do the djed of solidarity square with the idea of balance? Does the teacher mean that our attachment to the god, that is, the good, the object of the good, goodness, and godliness, obliterate sorrow, pain, and suffering? No, he means rather that solidarity to the god brings its own stability, its own rewards even if we experience pain and suffering.

Judgment: One can ascertain that judgment is the good sense to know that one should not discriminate since the beggar and the king must be viewed as one. Indeed, the wise understand that gold and dross are as one. This does not mean that there are no intrinsic differences but rather that one should not use difference as a means of discrimination. In fact, the real idea behind the philosopher's dictum is that the person has a view of life that insulates him or her from making undue judgments. Furthermore, one should not take right actions to please someone of high status, but because they are right actions.

The six djeds of Kagemni's instruction must not be seen as simply the creation of an individual. What the author produced as the six djeds was the collective wisdom of his day. He was the mouthpiece for the generally held beliefs of the Egyptian people. They knew by experience and observation and they believed by virtue of their cosmogony that certain "pillars" were a part of the reality of a people's existence and it was impossible for them to deny what they knew and what they believed. Kagemni, however, the student and judge, was instructed that human beings needed to be reminded of their duties to each other and their duties to God. Only by considering *devotion, compassion, loyalty, balance, solidarity, and judgment* could humans complete their destinies on earth and be assured of eternal life.

Additional fragments from the Kagemni seboyet give further indication of his judgment and wisdom regarding human relations:

On Propriety in Speech

The humble remains united with the people and the one who deals righteously with people is praised. The humble will find shelter and the speaker who uses propriety will find a comfortable place, but the one who strays from the path will find a sharp knife. Nothing could be more precious to teach than the concept of propriety. What is appropriate has a lot to do with balance, harmony, good sense, and tradition. In speech, the person who shortens the distance between his or her words and the people's understanding is considered a master at speech. Much later than Kagemni's unknown teacher it would be said of Jesus that without a parable he never spoke. This was a statement of Jesus' sense of propriety. It was something recognized in the Kagemni instructions centuries before Jesus.

On Social Graces at Meals

If you sit with many persons, do not show that you want to devour the food; it takes only a few moments to control one's self, and it is disgraceful to be greedy. A cup of water quenches thirst and if one's mouth be full of gratitude it strengthens the heart. A simple thing takes the place of that which is good just as little takes the place of much. He is a miserable man who is greedy because he shows no sense of propriety nor respect for others.

Be Cautious of Boastfulness

Do not boast of your strength in the midst of your own age group. Be on guard against any who will test you. You will never know what may happen just as you do not know how God punishes. The person who boasts draws negative, not positive, attention to himself or herself. Such negative attention is the source of much harm.

The text appears to be a straightforward enough ethical text, but like all Egyptian texts it is meant to be activated. Just as the priests had to activate the gods every day, the society had to be activated through the presentation of the six djeds. Here near the beginning of the dynastic period of Egypt, we find already the fundamental principles of the society being discussed by one of its highest officials. The author surely knows that these principles are based on the First Occasion and he is as dutiful and attentive to maintaining Maat as anyone, but he also knows that to be able to advance one's ideas it is necessary to reinforce the First Occasion with practical precepts.

CHAPTER SIX: MERIKARE ON COMMON SENSE

Good common sense has always been one of the marks of a mature person. Merikare's seboyet is one of the best examples of prescriptions for common sense. There is an 18th Dynasty copy of the seboyet that is the only such copy in existence. Most authorities believe that it comes from an earlier date, perhaps as early as the Old Kingdom, but certainly during the chaotic period between the Old and Middle Kingdoms. Merikare was probably one of the kings of Herakleopolis who ruled at a time when there was a simultaneous kingship at Thebes. The times were confused. Thus the kings of the 11th Dynasty at Thebes are contemporaneous with the monarchs of Herakleopolis. The name of Merikare's father who presents his wisdom to him is unknown to us. We know, of course, that the father himself is a king, but little else do we find about the man in the text. But what is the teaching?

The Value of Speaking Well

Be an artist in public speaking, so that you may prevail, for the power of a man is the tongue, and speech is mightier than any fighting. He that is skilled at speech, the sensible will not attack, if he is sensible, and no harm happens to the skillful.

Humans have always appreciated the good communicator and the early Egyptians had a high regard for the person who could speak well. It is no wonder that Merikare calls the good public speaker an artist because eloquence is based on the judicious use of language, propriety of tropes and metaphors, and the sincerity with which a person delivers a speech.

Be Benevolent, but Prudent

Be not evil, it is good to be kind. Cause your monument to endure forever because people love you. Men thank God on your account and they praise your goodness and pray for your health. Honor the great and prosper the people; good is it to work for the future. But keep your eyes open so that one who is trusting will not become a victim.

The prescription is simple and is based on the idea that if one does good instead of evil the benefits will be great. Merikare knows that the model for goodness is deeply planted in the Kemetic soul and that all one had to do was to appeal to the *tep zepi,* the First Occasion, and the text would be clear about how good was always the victor over evil, even if it took 80 years. It is not just good to be kind but to ensure that your monuments will endure forever. In addition, people will love you and pray to God on your behalf.

Behavior of a King

Do right so long as you live on earth. Calm the weeper, oppress no widow, expel no man from the possessions of his father, and do not harm the judges because of their roles. Be careful that you do not punish wrongfully. Slaughter not, because it does not profit you; punish with beatings and imprisonment. God knows the really evil person, God requites his sins in blood. Do not slay the person with whom you have chanted the sacred scriptures.

How could a king, one who is god on the earth, not listen to the wisdom of a great teacher? The role of the king as god was to make certain that Maat ruled in the earth. If justice, righteousness, order, harmony, truth, balance, and reciprocity did not exist in the land then the king must be held responsible. To rule justly and to rule effectively, Merikare lists a few practical considerations. One can see that each of these prescriptions is based on common sense.

On the Treatment of Youth

Train your young troops that the people may love you and secure you great respect. The young generation is happy following what is right.

Remember Piety

Exalt not the son of one of high degree more than him of lowly birth, but reward a person because of his actions. Practice every craft. Make monuments for God; they cause the name of the builder to live again. A person should do that which profits the soul in that he performs the monthly services and should put on white sandals, enter the temple, uncover the mysteries, enter the holiest places, and eat the bread of the temple.

One should cause the drink-table to be replenished, and present many loaves. Increase the permanent offering because it is profitable to him who does that. Cause your monuments to flourish, so long as you have strength. A single day given to eternity and hour does good to futurity. God knows the person who works for him.

Piety Towards Predecessors

The kingship is a Godly calling. Although one has no son and no brother who may cause the remembrance thereof to endure, yet one restores the monuments of the other kings. Each one does it for one that went before because he desires that what he himself has done may be maintained by another that comes after him.

Finally, God knows every name. Listen, I have spoken unto you the best of my inner thoughts; of course, you will act according to what has been established in your presence.

Merikare

CHAPTER SEVEN: SEHOTEPIBRE ON LOYALTY

Sehotepibre appears as a count, prince, and royal seal bearer to two kings in succession, Senusert III and Amenemhat III. Obviously Sehotepibre was well known in the court circles and influenced many people. While we only know about his functions and roles from what he said about himself and from what appears on the stela erected in Abydos, from all indications, in that document he was well regarded and had much to say about the conduct of society. His interest in the right attitude toward life, protocol, leadership, and loyalty led me to include his work in this volume. Both King Khakaure Senusert III and King NiMaatre Amenemhat III were 12th Dynasty rulers, between 1990 and 1785 BC. This was one of Kemet's Golden Periods when the rulers and the people made progress on the technical, architectural, and philosophical fronts. Sehotepibre demonstrates that he was a loyalist, a nationalist, a patriot of his country. Of course, serving as he did in the waning years of the dynasty he was intent on creating a legacy of loyalty in others and much of what he says in his seboyet had to do with allegiances.

An Introduction of Sehotepibre
In a most extraordinary introduction of himself, Sehotepibre provides his readers with an elaborate statement of his importance:

The Prince, Count, Royal Seal-Bearer, beloved Sole Companion, Great One of the King of Upper Kemet, Grandee of the King of Lower Kemet; Magistrate at

61

the head of the people. Overseer of horn, hoof, feather, scale, and swimming pools, whose coming is awaited by courtiers; to whom people confide their affairs; whose worth the lord of the Two Lands knows; whom he established as authority between the two banks. Keeper of silver and gold, Herdsman of all kinds of cattle; man of justice before the Two Lands; straight and true like Djehuty. Master of secrets in the temples; overseer of all the works of the king's house; more accurate than the plummet; the equal of the scales. Patient, effective in counsel; who says what is good, repeats what pleases; whose patience is unequaled; good at listening, excellent at speaking, An official who unravels what is knotty; whom his lord distinguished before millions. Truly exemplary and beloved; free of wrongdoing. Single-minded for the lord who has tried him; pillar of the South in the king's house; who follows his lord in his strides; his intimate before the courtiers. Who attends his lord alone; companion of Horus in the palace; true favorite of his lord; to whom secrets are told; who solves knotty problems, eases pain; acts for the best. The Royal Seal-bearer, Temple Overseer, Deputy Chief Seal-Bearer, Sehotepibre.*

What we know is that here is a man who thinks highly of himself and is not ashamed to say so. But we also know that there are those who would contest him if he spoke wrongly. Therefore, this panegyric to himself, while elaborate and perhaps overstated for contemporary readers, is considered by Sehotepibre to be a fair representation of his place in the society. Even more, he has demonstrated that his relationship with the king is close and that when the king speaks it is very much like what he would say himself; he is the sole companion of the king. While Sehotepibre erected the stela during the reign of Amenemhat, it bore an inscripted titulary to Senusert as well.

Although there is considerable discussion of his autobiographical information and obviously Sehotepibre was engaged in a constructive relationship with royalty, he was also interested in leaving instructions, wisdom, the seboyet, for posterity. Thus, he laid down in a formulary way some of the principal tenets of his own beliefs about good conduct for his children:

I am going to let you hear something great
I am giving you eternal counsel
About right conduct in life and living in peace:
Worship King NiMaatre, ever-living in your bodies
Hold to His Majesty in your hearts!
He is Sia in the hearts,
His eyes seek out everyone,
He is Ra who sees with his rays,
He lights the Two Lands more than the sun-disk,
Who makes the land green more than Great Hapi
He has filled the Two Lands with life force.
Noses turn cold when he starts to rage,
When he is at peace one breathes air.
He gives food to those who serve him,
He nourishes him who treads his path.

The king is sustenance, his mouth is plenty
He who will be is his creation.
He is the Khnum of everybody
Begetter who makes mankind.
He is Bastet who guards the Two Lands,

He who worships him is sheltered by his arm
He is Sekhmet to him who defies his command
He who he hates will bear distress
Fight for his name, respect his oath
Then you stay free of betrayal
The king's beloved will be honored
His Majesty's enemy has no tomb
His corpse is tossed into the water
Do this, then you prosper.
It will serve you forever.

Listen to this, what is Sehotepibre really saying to his children? This is an instruction in loyalty.

Loyalty seems like a rather old-fashioned value in our society. So what is loyalty anyway? It is an attitude of solidarity with another person, usually one who has benefited you greatly in some form or fashion. But there is more here than simple loyalty to the king. One must understand how the ancient Africans felt about kingship to fully appreciate Sehotepibre's instructions in this matter. The king represented more than himself; the king carried the ka force of the nation and this force was the source of the collective solidarity of the people. To be in solidarity with the king, that is, to be loyal to the king, is in actuality to be in solidarity with one's self and fellows.

In many traditional African societies one can still find this view of the kingship today. For example, among the Akan people of Ghana, the king is the repository of the energy of the ancestors, the direct linkage to the meaning of the nation, to the sacredness of the collective union of the society. If something should happen to the king, then it happens to the rest of the society. A strong king means a strong people; a weak king means a weak people.

Inasmuch as Heru was the royal symbol, as defined in the First Occasion, the people accepted the fact that the king in his Heru role was the embodiment of the ka force. To destroy the king is to destroy the ka force. For the ancient Egyptian the affection for the king was not merely an affection for a man, but an affection for the ka force which transcended a particular person, place, or time but was temporarily embodied in the king whom people saw.

A king is as strong as the ka force. One could, by identifying with Heru, attain a certain degree of this ka power as well. It was only restricted to the king in the sense that he represented the collective consciousness; others could rise to an appreciation of their own ka force. But the principal point that I am making is that the encouragement to loyalty must be seen in the light of the overall Egyptian philosophy and not be isolated as something merely secular.

Sehotepibre's instruction is useful because it reminds us that there was an interdependence that was crucial to the Egyptian society. The king's ka force supported the nation and in an hierarchical society it was also true that the ka force of those nobles who had attained a level of consciousness supported in turn their own followers and supporters. Evidence from the Valley of the Kings suggests that the nobles, many of whom were adepts and prophets, used their ka force to establish a kind of bond between them and their followers. They practiced calling upon the ancestors in such a way that like Pepi they could say,

"Things are well with me and my name
I live by my ka,
It destroys the evil before me
It destroys the evil behind me."

The ka force was mainly conceived of as a universal and collective idea when viewed in connection with loyalty to the king. What is it to be loyal to the king if it is not to be loyal to one's ka force and hence to the larger ka force of the nation?

Sehotepibre's admonitions about loyalty therefore must be seen in connection with the way the universal order was in the First Occasion. The gods established the pattern of loyalty by being supporters of Heru against the supporters of Set. And although there were times when the situation was in flux, the idea of ka of the Heru being supported by the company of deities was certainly established in the First Occasion. So here, in this instruction, Sehotepibre is not merely calling upon a secular, literal loyalty but the protection and the sustenance of the society and indeed the world. This is why he is able to say, "The king is sustenance, his mouth is plenty." The integral connection of the ka of the king with the sustaining of the society and the world—and ultimately, through the various manifestations of the deities, the universe—is a real and powerful bond.

Sehotepibre is not writing out of ignorance of how the universe functions. He knows that all systems of governance, all loyalties, and all protection are essentially in the realm of the First Occasion during the realization of the cosmos. The three aspects of the cosmos: the earth itself, the sky above the earth, and the region between the earth and the sky are intertwined in some ways and the interpenetration of one by the other as well as the gateway to each of them is controlled by the person of the king. This is why the king is the Sa Ra, the son of God, and why he is the Ra who sees with his rays. But these are not simply material spaces that exist apart from humans. It is a world of symbols constituted to retain the order and the balance of the universe. This is unlike the later Western notion of trying to keep the balance of nature, because nature is only one part of the universe, and the ancient Africans believed that if you demonstrated loyalty to the king's ka you would, in effect, be working to maintain the entire universe which included the three cosmological regions but also the personalities that are modeled on the First Occasion principles.

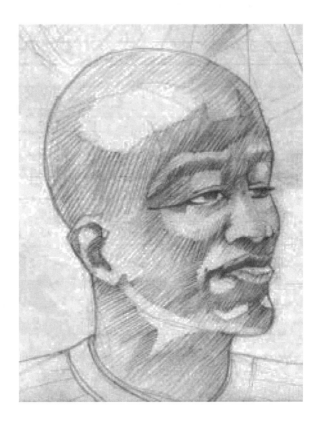

Sehotepibre

CHAPTER EIGHT: AMENEMHAT SINGS THE BLUES

The book of Amenemhat was obviously one of the more favorite texts in ancient Egypt. During the New Kingdom it was very popular and there are at least four different papyri of the text and portions of the text are found in about ten ostraca.

When one considers the facts surrounding this seboyet it is clear that it represents a philosophical statement about how one should conduct one's life. Amenemhat I (1991–1962 BC), during the 20th year of his reign, made his son, Senusert I, co-regent and then withdrew from public life. The major text tells of the old king, Amenemhat, recounting to Senusert I, by way of admonitions, warnings, and precepts, the events that led to him taking the steps to abandon political life. The aged king had been betrayed and an attempted assassination had been foiled.

Seboyet, which the majesty of the King Sehotepibre the son of Ra, Amenemhat, made in a message to his son, Senusert, the Lord of All.

He says: You who have appeared as divine, listen to what I shall say to you so that you may be king over the land, and ruler over the river banks, and that you may do more good than expected. Be on your guard against subordinates; do not approach them, and be not alone. Trust not a brother, know not a friend, and make not for yourself intimates, that action profits nothing.

The Egyptian Philosophers:
Ancient African Voices from Imhotep to Akhenaten

If you sleep, make sure you guard your own heart because in the day of adversity a man has no adherents. I gave to the poor and nourished the orphan, I caused him that was nothing to reach the goal, even the one who was of little account.

It was the one who ate my food who disdained me; it was the one whom I gave my hand that aroused fear with the kindness I showed. They that clothed them in my fine linen looked at me as a shadow, and they that anointed them with my perfume, poured water.

My images are among the living, and my shares are in the offerings among men; and yet they contrived a conspiracy against me, without it being heard, and a great contest without it being seen. Men fought one day on the battlefield and forget my good deeds the next day. One does not have good fortune if he does not know what he ought to know.

It was after dinner when night had come; I had taken an hour of repose, and laid down upon my bed. I was weary and my heart began to follow after slumber. Then it was as if weapons were brandished, and as if one inquired concerning me and I became like a snake in the desert.

I awoke to fight alone and I noticed that it was a hand-to-hand affray of the bodyguard. When I had quickly taken weapons into my hand, I drove back the rogues. But there is no strength by night, and one cannot fight alone, and success does not come without you to protect me.

*Listen, the abominable thing came to pass when
I was without you, when the Court had not yet heard
that I am resigning the sovereign power to you when
you and I did not dwell together. May I act according
to your counsels for I fear the courtiers no more and I
am powerless against the indolence of servants?*

*Had the women set the battle in array? Had
the conflict been fostered within the house? Were the
townspeople made foolish on account of the deeds of
the conspirators? Ill fortune has not come to me since
my birth and nothing has happened that might equal
my prowess as a doer of good deeds.*

There is a sense of tremendous sadness in the tone of
Amenemhat because he had given so much and had received so
little from those around him. His bitterness was not unnatural
and he was unable to pull himself up from the depths of cynicism. Whether all he said he had done or believed that he had
done was correct or not, one cannot tell; however, it is possible
to state that given the magnitude of his achievements and the
richness of his life he had impacted lots of people. His disap-
pointments had come because he expected more of those whom
he had assisted.

Is this not the story of human life? Does not this tale
ring true for contemporary situations as well? Amenemhat's
story sounds like one of B. B. King's blues songs. Amenemhat
is the original Blues Singer, expressing his sadness about the
things he has experienced. For example, the loss of a friend,
loneliness, poverty, betrayal, and ingratitude are enough to make
one want to cry. B. B. King named his guitar "Lucille" because
it reminded him of a woman who had disappointed him.
Amenemhat may have had a harp, the ancient guitar, as he told
his story of pain.

Amenemhat's instructions are for success as he sees it. His own experience was enough to convince him that those who are closest to you are often the ones who bring you the most pain. At least, that was his experience.

His cynicism ran deeply. In fact, he tells the student not to trust a brother, avoid making friends, and make no intimates because that action will bring you nothing. If this is not the most distant assessment of friendship then what else is possible? His observations are like those of many humans. He believed that one must secure himself when sleeping because when you are in trouble you will have no friends. "In the day of adversity a man has no adherents," he writes. This is the time your "friends" abandon you and move on to someone else. Those who were around you as confidantes now become your accusers. Those who once told you how great you were now condemn you without knowing the facts. They are the vultures who surround you to attack your corpse.

It does not matter that you have given much, that you have supported others, that you have risked your profession and career to advance others. Amenemhat gave to the poor, nourished the orphan, and caused him of little account to reach his goal, and yet he was abandoned. It reminds one of the Blues song, "When I had a good job, I would help anybody/when I had a job I would help any friend of mine/when I had a job I would help anybody/but now that I am broke and need a job, I can't get a lousy dime."

The Blues singer says, "Take a fool's advice, don't you loan all of your money to your friends/Take my advice, don't give all your money to your friends/You can have lots of money/ but now look at the shape I'm in." The bards along the Mississippi had the most intense encounter with reality. They were the descendants of those who had worked on the plantations. Some still worked on the plantations in the 20th century, and they knew how bad humans could be. The making of the Blues was an engagement with reality, face to face. Most of what disturbed the Blues singer was the way humans treated each other. If your girlfriend or boyfriend misuses you, then you can get the blues. If you have done all that you can to assist someone, to aid them when they had the blues, or to lift the veil of sadness from their face—and then they hurt you, you'll get the blues. Why would someone turn on the person who had done the most to advance them? This is the age-old question.

Amenemhat was disappointed by those who ate his food and yet disdained him, and by those who had been anointed with his perfume and later gave him water. In the end, when he was attacked in the night he had to fight alone. And though he fought like a snake in the desert he knew that one could not fight a cadre of rogues alone.

The lessons of Amenemhat are abundantly clear. One cannot depend upon successes in life to guarantee friendship. Regardless of how much one gives to others, there will be those who will abandon you in times of distress. Most people do not like adversity and run away from those who are having it. They believe that to support those who are in distress, particularly those who have had much success but find themselves in trouble, is to invite distress to themselves.

Amenemhat's message was clear. He had tamed lions and conquered crocodiles, defeated armies and carried off prisoners, but that did not ensure that he would be loved or respected. No one can guarantee friendship or intimates. In the end the person must allow his or her works to speak to posterity since those around us can be extremely fickle.

Amenemhat

CHAPTER NINE: KHUNANUP: CLASS AND MAAT

Khunanup was a peasant of the Wadi Natron. He was married to Marye. This much we know from the manuscript often called the "Eloquent Peasant," a document of 430 lines. Preserved in papyrus from the Middle Kingdom Period (2040–1650BC) extant copies of the text are P. Berlin 3023 (B1), P. Berlin 3025 (B2), P. Berlin 10499 (R), and a fourth copy at the British Museum, P. Butler 527.

Who created this text is not known. I have called it the Seboyet of Khunanup after the name of the peasant in the text. The elegance of the arguments in the text speaks to a reflective and studied concentration of the nature of human relationships, greed, honor, respect, authority, power, poverty, generosity, and punishment. The tension between the rhetorical artifice and skill of Khunanup and the silence of Rensi, the magistrate, gives this text a strong contemporary message in achieving justice. It is always difficult to bring the strong before the bar of justice because power builds on power and only the moral will and determination of the weak can overcome, if ever, the position of the strong. The lessons of this text, the Seboyet of Khunanup, are concrete and encouraging.

Kemet remains for us the model civilization in antiquity because it provides, more than any other civilization at a comparable time, information, documents, scripts, sculptures, and other accounts of its prodigious creations. Here we are confronted with the very evidence of the emergence of our consciousness, and hence, our use of the artifice of communication. There are few examples more precise about the nature of Maat in human relationships than the story of Khunanup, a peasant who appeals to magistrates for justice in a case where he was robbed and beaten. The appeal of Khunanup is one of profound speech, divine speech.

If St. John says that "In the beginning was the word, and the word was with God," then the first humans to record that word as an aspect of the divine were the Egyptians in Africa.

I argue here that reverence for the word, based as it was on the future life, was the source of the Egyptian's concern with Maat and precision in language. Thus, when we examine Khunanup's story we are at the very frontier of appreciating the immense world of good and evil. This seems to be reflected in the development of cosmogonies that showed the origin of things out of the four aspects: light, life, land, and consciousness. But these were themselves derived from water, the primeval source. And hence, the Greek philosophers, the Ionian mainly, followed in this tradition until the appearance of the Athenians who attempted to modify the lessons of the ancient Africans.

The appearance of Shu, the first Dawn, is the separation of sky and earth, where the coming of the light is the introduction of the word into the world. Life emerges as a flower that reveals its light with the opening of its petals. Land is the primeval mound. Consciousness is revealed in the mastery of mind and will over self, and thus origin must be seen in the sense of the biblical, indeed pre-biblical "in the beginning was the word" because the word is at the heart of will, understanding, command, and persuasion.

Ancient Egyptians did not have one view of cosmogony, that is, the structure of the universe. They had at least three interpretations of the universe and each one was connected to the word. It is, however, the creative spirit of Ptah where we see the world spoken into existence. All things came into existence by the word of Ptah. On the other hand, Atum ejaculated into his own hand and by his semen created the world. Ra, as Khepera, also is credited with the creation of all things. These are manifestations of the great myth of creation.

Perhaps one reason there was never a canonical rendering of the creation story in ancient Kemet was the fact that the word was so mysterious that it could not be dealt with simply. As one spoke the word one spoke that which was divine and thus created the world, the beginning, each time the word was spoken. But maybe it is not mystery, that is, the inexplicable, that we should see in the word, but divinity, the source and end of all mystery. This is why the Egyptians called their language the Mdu Ntr, Medu Netcher, the Divine Words. It is from this understanding that the Greeks gave us the term hieroglyphics, literally the "sacred carvings." Words were like the divine as well as being divine themselves. What one said was in essence so important and so real that it was sacred.

Words had real implications for the next life, and therefore had to be spoken and recorded perfectly. The ancient Egyptians believed that death was essential to all life. Indeed, death was a prelude to life. This was the polarity of existence; one stage was meaningless without the other, as Rundle Clark says, and there was an alternation between one and the other among humans, animals, plants, and the stars. Death was moving from one plane of life to another plane of life. What is in the Dat (conveniently translated "the Underworld") is always becoming more perfect.

Forms are given which will later appear or reappear, and thus life is visible, becoming is invisible. The principal engine for this is the sun which itself must somehow disappear beyond the horizon to be refitted. All of this takes place beyond the reach of humans. The Dat is not reachable by the living. But it is the abode of Ausar, the recumbent, not Ausar, the Dead King, or the Spirit of Fertility or the God of Inundation, but the keeper of *Iru (irw)*, form, shape, the making of the perfect. So complicated was the meaning of the Dat that the ancients gave us the Book of Caverns, the Book of the Two Ways, the Books of Gates, Coffin Text 336, the Book of What Is in the Dat, and the Book of the Dead, or the Book of the Going Forth by Day and the Coming Forth by Night. And it was Ausar who was the *neb tem*, the universal master, of this becoming in the Dat.

What can one say in practical everyday life that would make sense to the transformation that will occur in the Dat? How must one speak? As you can see these are not easy questions since everything we do in this life is reflected in the next, and the character of one's speech in this life will have implications for eternity. Of course, in current Western communication one can easily change what one said yesterday or delete it and start over again. It was more difficult I believe, for the Egyptian, and thus as we shall see, the incredible power of the Eloquent Peasant demonstrates a considerable skill and will.

The implications for communicating in a situation in which precision is required are enormous. One could say that the reverence for the word reverberated throughout everything that the society constructed and led to the stability which was a major force in maintaining **Maat.** When we are confronted with Maat we are confronted with the possibilities of establishing truth, harmony, righteousness, justice, order, balance, and reciprocity, for these are the elements that construct our response to the universe. It is not possible to choose one English word that is so pregnant with all the characteristics of this ancient concept. But yet it is at the heart of what we think when we imagine the nature of the Egyptian society as one of divine speech. As I reflect on this it reminds me of the Native Americans' concept and understanding of speech, the sacredness with which they held the word, their insistence, as among the Iroquois, that you allowed for a period of silence of maybe three minutes after a person spoke to permit her or him to change their minds after reflecting on what was just said. Well, the Africans had a similar idea in the ancient times and it went by the term **Maat** as a comprehensive concept including balance, harmony, order, righteousness, truth, justice, and reciprocity.

The Mystery System as Divine Word

Recently Mary Lefkowitz argued in her book *Not Out of Africa* that the concept of a mystery system was a Renaissance Affair, not truly something the Africans ought to be proud of since it was a fanciful creation of Europeans. Of course, like she has been on so many other things, Lefkowitz is incorrect about the system of mysteries as developed by the Egyptian priests. The priestly caste represented the intelligentsia of the ancient Egyptian society much like the professor class represents the vast majority of such a class today. Strabo, one of the major Greek writers of his time (58 BC to 25 AD), confirmed that the priests of Egypt attracted Greeks to study in Africa. Among the Greeks who benefitted from the instruction of the Africans were Plato and Eudoxus, both of whom spent thirteen years in Egypt. Strabo reports:

> **We were also shown Plato's and Eudoxus' dwellings for Eudoxus had accompanied Plato here, after arriving at Heliopolis, they stayed there for thirteen years among the priests. This fact is affirmed by several authors. These priests, so profoundly knowledgeable about celestial phenomena,**

were at the same time mysterious people, who did not talk much, and it is after a long time and with skillful maneuvering that Eudoxus and Plato were able to be initiated into some of their theoretical speculations. But these barbarians kept the best part to themselves. And if today the world owes them the knowledge of what fraction of a whole day has to be added to 365 whole days in order to have a complete year, the Greeks did not know the true duration of the year and many other facts of the same nature until translators of the Egyptian priests' papers into the Greek language popularized these notions among modern astronomers.

There were five main systems used by the priests to convey and conceal truth. These are normally referred to as the *Gemaria*, which is based on the numerical system of words, the *Temura*, by which a word reveals its power in its anagram, the transposition of letters, (e.g., Salem, Males), *Notarian,* a form of stenography, and there is also *Allegory*, the setting forth of truth from myths and parables. The fifth method was the use of sacerdotal language, the *Senzar*. To master such a system took considerable time and the Egyptians were very cautious in revealing their truths to foreigners. The priests were reserved to say the least and believed that it was necessary to keep the main portion of their secrets to themselves so they would not be in competition with their foreign students. Thus, they devised ways of communicating without giving all of their secrets away. One can see why Pythagoras had to spend 22 years in Egypt in order to study and even so the Egyptians did not give him all of the knowledge they possessed.

Maat is the principal concept that underlies the interrelations of humans with others and with the *neteru*. To say that the Egyptians used *Maat* as the basis for life is almost an understatement since it was fundamental to all communication and interaction. Thus the philosophy of the ancient Egyptians is filled with ethical principles related to Maat which included righteousness, truth, justice, balance, harmony, order and reciprocity. Since *Maat* is the mediating of the opposites or contrasting pairs in life, it means that specific individuals, institutions, and situations can be viewed *Maatically*. Actually the principle of creation is based on the union of opposites that give us existence. For example, a male cannot produce offspring alone; neither can a female. From observation the Egyptians knew that it took contrasting pairs to bring into existence good communication. Everywhere the Egyptian communicator looked he or she saw dualities, pairs, contrasts. There was light and dark, hot and cold, night and day, Ausar and Auset, male and female, and an endless world of dualities. Even when one had to express a truth in *mdw ntr* as in the writing on the tombs or in the temples, the idea was to show balance, harmony, and duality if possible. One can ascertain from this philosophy why it was easy for the ancient Egyptians to view life in terms of the strict demands of *Maat*. Thus, one spoke of those who were either good or bad, wise or foolish.

But *Maat* was expressed in both religious and philosophical terms. Innocent Onyewuenyi has called the two aspects of these terms Temple Thinking and Wisdom Thinking. I like to think of it as ethical and practical philosophy. The point is that the Egyptians held *Maat* as the basis of both Temple and Wisdom Thinking. In the ethical area one finds the discovery of *Maat* in the intellectual measures that posit the cosmogonies as outgrowths of the first cause. In the African sense the universe was not created out of chaos, but out of order and it is the responsibility of humans to do everything in their power to hold back the chaos on the margins. After all stability, order, and balance are essential to *Maat* and *Maat* is essential to maintaining the universe. This is why the pharaoh was the great bringer of *Maat*, stability and peace. His words, spoken carefully and with the authority of the gods, was divine speech itself, to be honored, carved into stone, and chiseled into the face of the mountains.

There were ten virtues that accompanied any representation of Maat in speech or behavior. They were:

1. **Criticality:** the ability to distinguish good from evil, and right from wrong. In the practice of Maat one was always aware of the ultimate rendezvous with the Dat. The people of Kemet thought of death as a prelude to life. That is precisely the reason why the stone crypt was called the *neb-ankh*, the Lord of Life. Death and life formed a polarity and one had no meaning without the other. Actually it is the moving from one type of time to another type of time that underscores what death is in the traditions of the ancients. It is necessary to test one's ability to distinguish the good from the evil, the day from the night, and one type of time from another type of time.

2. **Devotion:** Consecrating oneself by vow to Maat. How one consecrated oneself was based on the linkage to the spiritual rites. If a person was a devotee of one of the gods he would practice the rites necessary to demonstrate devotion, but devotion itself would only be revealed in the actual way a person responded to deep meditation.

An Egyptian, with great sincerity, came to a priest and asked, "What can I do to show devotion?"

The priest, obviously aware of the Khunanup story, said, "You cannot show devotion; it must arise in your own heart and even if others will not see it, you will know it."

3. **Control:** Regulate, check, and exercise power over the mind. Humans are born into order but remain oblivious to this order as chaos seems to penetrate our lives.

4. **Discipline.** Training that develops self control, orderly behavior.

5. **Tolerance:** Allowing and permitting others to express their views.

6. **Forbearance:** Possessing freedom from resentment.

7. **Steadfastness:** Holding firm to one's beliefs and ideas.

8. **Faith:** An expression of optimism.

9. **Spiritual Desire:** Showing the will to achieve victory over present circumstances.

10. **Initiation:** Achieving mastery over self.

Given the fact that this speech may be the earliest persuasive speech ever recorded, long before Pericles or Homer ever lived, it is important that we consider the extent to which the orator used the special principles of Maat. This text has been called the Story of the Eloquent Peasant for a very good reason. It is introduced by a narrative which frames the story. Nine speeches follow which speak to the issue at hand. The story has been called by Miriam Lichtheim a disquisition on the need for justice as well as an expression of the utility of eloquence.

The peasant Khunanup sets out on a road to trade in a distant city and is met by a man, Nemtynakht, who covets the goods he is carrying. On one side of the house was his barley fields and on the other side was the river. When Khunanup approached Nemtynakht's house, his donkeys could not go around one way or the other because on one side was the steep river bank and on the other side was Nemtynakht's barley fields. Khunanup's donkeys started around the sheet and through the barley, and one of the asses ate a wisp of barley. Nemtynakht accused the peasant of violating his property and demanded that the donkey belonged to him to pay off the debt of eating from Nemtynakht's barley. The peasant protested pointing out how difficult it had been since Nemtynakht had laid the sheet in the path. Nevertheless Nemtynakht succeeded in taking the peasant's donkeys, goods, and food. He was stripped to nothing. After ten days of beseeching Nemtynakht to no avail, the peasant decided to go to Rensi, the son of Meru, and ask for justice. He was the representative of the pharaoh. Rensi heard the case and was pleased with the words of the peasant. Rensi called Nemtykahkt and took his goods and gave them to Khunanup.

Khunanup was a peasant. This is remarkable and shows that a simple man, a farmer with no special schooling or pedigree, could create a speech demanding Maat. The Egyptian society thus elevates the common oratory of a peasant to the highest form of the struggle.

Khunanup's confrontation was with a rich man. Nemtynakht possessed large barley fields and was well connected, yet it becomes the speech of Khunanup that makes a difference to Rensi. There are values of respect, dignity, wisdom, and eloquence in the peasant's precise speech.

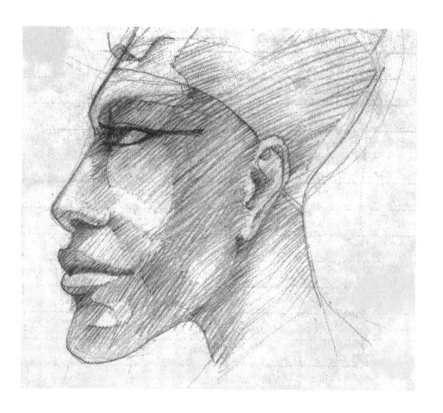

Khunanup

The Egyptian Philosophers:
Ancient African Voices from Imhotep to Akhenaten

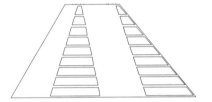

CHAPTER TEN: AMENHOTEP, SON OF HAPU: CONTEMPLATION AND ITS REWARDS

One of the most striking sculptures in the Luxor Museum is that of Amenhotep, the son of Hapu, sitting in the lotus position with a writing pad in his hand. This is the first image of the thinker to be portrayed in history. Long before Rodin ever conceived of the thinker, a great African sculptor looking into history brought Amenhotep alive in stone.

Few humans ever achieved the stature of Amenhotep, son of Hapu, as a deified being. Alongside Imhotep, who preceded him by many centuries, Amenhotep, son of Hapu, an architect and philosopher, was made a god by the Egyptian people.

Like Imhotep and Kagemni, to whom he has been compared, Amenhotep, son of Hapu, was an officer. He served during the 18th Dynasty. Since Amenhotep III was considered one of the greatest builders in Egyptian history, most of the reign of Amenhotep III was spent in building or restoring monuments, temples, and palaces.

Amenhotep, son of Hapu, was revered because he represented in his person and profession the embodiment of the ancient traditions. Obviously knowledgeable of the scientific and mathematical foundations of much of Egyptian architecture and sculpture, Amenhotep became accepted as a philosopher, a wise man, a sage. He was respected by the royal court as one of the wisest of men and it is said that he was known as a learned man, one of culture, who had shown all of the sacred books and beheld the excellencies of Djehuty. Participating in the divine nature of Djehuty he had also written a book of magic thus projecting the traditional wisdom and knowledge for the benefit of a larger public. It was this public presentation of his inner knowledge, of his wisdom, that gave him the image of a sharer of information. Like all architects he was a priest and could serve as the kheri-heb, reciting magical formulas from memory, or could, as he did, originate formulas on the basis of his great breadth of knowledge.

His king, Amenhotep III, considered him so magnificent as a human being and wise counselor that he ordered the establishment of a statue in his honor for the Temple of Amen at Karnak even in his lifetime. This was never done before and even Imhotep, as far as we know, did not have this type of reverence from his king, Djoser. Beyond the setting up of the statue and the ritual that went with it, Amenhotep III saw to it that mortuary provisions were made for the care of Amenhotep, son of Hapu's own tomb on the west bank of the Nile in perpetuity.

When Alexander the Macedonian conquered Egypt in 333 BC, he left his general Ptolemy in charge of the country. In time, the Ptolemaic Dynasty would establish control over the country and try to integrate the Greek occupiers into the customs of Africa. In fact, Ptolemy IV had a temple built at Deir el Medina adjacent to the tomb of Amenhotep, son of Hapu's grave to pay homage to someone already considered a deity. The grave site was said to be sacred even prior to the arrival of the Greeks. But we can see that Ptolemy did not see anything wrong with the worship of Amenhotep, son of Hapu, nor the worship of Imhotep, who was worshipped in the same temple as Amenhotep, son of Hapu. As Imhotep had been associated with Ptah and Sekhmet, Amenhotep was closely related to Amen-Ra and Ausar and was worshipped at Karnak alongside them. He was represented as a bearded man holding a papyrus roll.

One of the keys to understanding the mind of the ancient philosophers is the work they performed and the time that they performed it. Amenhotep, son of Hapu, was always associated with a book or a papyrus roll. One gathers the idea that he was committed to the intellectual life although he was awfully busy with the affairs of state, particularly the construction of the temples and monuments ordered by his king. However, this gives us a penetrating look into the philosophical problems that must have confronted such an individual. For example, the issues of motion, reality, and space are very real to an architect, especially one who must work with fundamental substances each day. How can we get into the unconscious presumptions of the philosopher who lived so long ago?

We know, for instance, that Amenhotep, son of Hapu, was also gifted in magic and had written a magic book. But one who writes such a book has some appreciation for the rudiments of science because in so many ways magic is applied science. There is little that is mystical about what the magician achieves. A certain train of events is set into motion by the vocal rendering of the formulas. Sequences are established which allow other sequences to follow. Magic is achieved when the sequences go smoothly and one does not know that magic has been performed. Fundamental to the way the ancient Egyptian philosopher Amenhotep, son of Hapu, approached magic was the spoken word. The generative and productive quality of the spoken word is powerful in a way that is not possible to see or behold outside of an African American event. No magic can exist apart from the spoken word, but once the word is spoken it is possible to resolve all human and superhuman conflicts, to overcome the problems of space and distance.

Amenhotep, son of Hapu, becomes the world's first iconic example of a scholar. When ancient artists depicted him, more than any of the other philosophers, they showed him to be a devotee of knowledge and therein is the longevity of Amenhotep, son of Hapu's fame.

Yet it is in Amenhotep, son of Hapu's insistence on the Maatian ethics that distinguishes him as a philosopher. His belief in Maat was equal to Kagemni's. For Maat was not simply the visualization of a philosophical concept but a real, practical idea in the time of Amenhotep, son of Hapu. The physical form of Maat was as a woman carrying the sceptre and an ankh; she wore an ostrich feather in her hair. But the philosophical concept and the practical idea were both considered Maat, essentially meaning truth, justice, balance, harmony, righteousness, and reciprocity. Herein is the key to understanding how Amenhotep, son of Hapu, must have viewed his duties and responsibilities and those of his fellow citizens. For it is in Maat that all ethical behavior for humans is based. After death, Maat is again active in the judgment. It is a proper ordering and construction of the individual, society, and the universe, maintaining what is correct, just, and meaningful in human behavior.

One common interpretation of Maat is straightness. This idea gained popularity because some of the earliest glyphs representing Maat suggested intersecting straight lines; thus, to be Maat is to be straight. In Burkina Faso, a contemporary West African country, the name of the nation represents a continuation of the idea of straightness inasmuch as the name means "straight people." Maat brings straightness out of chaos, order out of confusion. And for philosophers like Amenhotep, son of Hapu, the belief in the gods had real implications for social behavior. If one could accept Maat, the daughter of God, the Lady of Heaven, as divine, then one could see the potential in accepting other humans for their divine qualities. Indeed, as one text says, Maat has not been disturbed since the days of creation.

It would take a figure as profoundly ethical in the traditions of the Egyptians as Amenhotep, son of Hapu, to know that the goddess Maat was only the embodiment of ideas that reached all the way back to the emergence of Ra in the primeval waters.

Maat was coexistent with the Almighty. In the Coffin Texts there is the story that Maat and Ra were brought together so that Maat might have an influence on Ra. When a tired, old Ra asked Nun for advice, Nun told him to kiss Maat and regain vitality. *The Book of the Coming Forth By Day and Going Forth By Night* states that Maat and Tehuti appeared in Heru's presence on Ra's solar boat.

By virtue of his high status in the pantheon of humans who have become divine, I am convinced that Amenhotep, son of Hapu, was a paragon of Maat himself. Indeed Maat's philosophical bearing was the highest level of wisdom, truth, and justice. The life of Amenhotep, son of Hapu, as the architect and chief advisor to Amenhotep III, was a reflection of the great architectural monuments of Kemet: beautiful, harmonious, and balanced.

During and after the New Kingdom period, Amenhotep, son of Hapu, represented the symbol of reflection. In his pose as scholar, thinker, and philosopher, he embodied the best elements of the Kemetic character and was honored by the elite as well as the ordinary people. Amenhotep, son of Hapu, was the quintessential Kemetic person, devoted to the gods, to the nation, and to a life of Maat.

The secret to Amenhotep, son of Hapu's ascendancy as a spiritual force in Kemet is his belief in the wholistic nature of the universe. For Amenhotep, nothing happened that was not connected to something else. And since all that was connected was a part of the same fabric of life, wants, desires, ambitions, sadnesses, and joys, the human being was intricately intertwined with all others. To believe in the same spiritual force as the rest of humanity is to organize a powerful energy. Amenhotep marshaled the forces of integrity, goodness, and honesty in the service of the spiritual.

91

Amenhotep

CHAPTER ELEVEN: DUAUF ON LOVING BOOKS

The great renown of Duauf is based on his quest for the true meaning of things. Thus he becomes one of the first teachers to seek the meaning of the substantial even though his special power lay in the use of satire. As the son of Khety, the great scribe, he exhibited an outstanding breadth of knowledge and protocol in terms of the professions. Using all of the knowledge at his disposal and to which he had been exposed, Duauf made his instructions for his son Pepi.

A course of instructions, referred to often as wisdom literature, was often required of the sons of those who would serve the country in the role of scribes, priests, or professionals. Thus, there grew in Egypt the belief that such future leaders ought to have some specific guidance since there were no "revealed texts" to guide them.

Of course, the greater the preparation of the teacher in the history, culture, and protocols of the society, the better the instructions he will provide to others. Duauf was influenced by the Kemetian relationship to land, which gave rise to the values and beliefs that defined their interpersonal and business relationships. The cosmogonies and systems of thought emerging from this type of social condition would have a basically humanistic pattern to them. A naturalistic type of thinking, that is, a speculation about the composition of human values, lives, professions, and of the universe, would give someone a definite orientation to human relationships. Duauf's work was based in the general Egyptian pattern of critical thinking.

Striking advances in systematic thinking was possible after Duauf. He presented a special way of viewing the relationship between professional categories of people. While the Greeks would come and be consumed by the need for an abstract understanding of the universe, the Kemites felt the need to advance human understanding in much the same vein as the Chinese philosophers would later feel. The works of Confucius, Mencius, and Chu Hsi show a startling similarity to the Egyptian philosophers although the work of the Egyptians came thousands of years before. A diffusionist might reflect on the origin and the extension of African philosophy to other parts of the world.

It is fitting that we turn to the text to gain a flavor of Duauf's wisdom that was written between the Old and Middle Kingdom. He said to his son Pepi, "I have seen him that is beaten, you are to set your heart on books. I have beheld him that is set free from forced labor: behold, nothing surpasses books." Already we are face to face with a remarkable statement about ancient Egypt. There is a sense here, even in satire where it exists, that the philosopher of ancient Egypt is concerned that the youth read books. Nothing surpasses books, whether it is a fact of life or not in the Old and Middle Kingdom, it is believed that books are important.

Duauf reminds his son of what happens to all of the professions. He cites a long list of professions and their possible pitfalls. He speaks on the sculptor, the goldsmith, the blacksmith, the barber, the builder, the gardener, the farmer, and others. In the end, he still believes that delving into books is more valuable than anything else one could do. He wants to make his son love books more than his mother. This is why he details the life of every one of his colleagues who tries to create trouble. The text is clear:

> Read at the end of the Kemet and you find this sentence: The scribe, his is every place at the residence and he knows what he is doing. But the one who acts according to the understanding of another does not have success. The other professions are as this sentence says.
>
> I would like to make you love books more than your momma; I would like to bring their beauty right in front of your face. It is greater than any calling.
>
> I have never seen a sculptor on an errand nor a goldsmith as he was being sent forth. But I have seen the smith at his task at the mouth of his furnace. His fingers were like stuff from crocodiles, he stank more than the offal of fishes.
>
> Every artisan who wields the chisel is wearier than he who delves into books; his field is the wood and his hoe is the metal. In the night when he is set free, he works beyond what the arm can do; in the night he burns a light.
>
> The stone-mason seeks work in all types of hard stone. When he completes it, his arms are destroyed and he is weary. When such a one sits down at dusk his thighs and his back are broken.
>
> The barber shaves late into the evening, going from street to street, seeking someone to shave. He strains his arm in order to fill his stomach, like a bee feeds at its work.

The small bricklayer with the Nile mud spends his life among the cattle; he is concerned with swine and vines, his clothes are stiff, he works with his feet, pounding.

The gardener brings loads and his arm and neck are sore from the weight. In the morning he waters the leek, and at evening, the vines.

The field-worker's reckoning endures forever; he has a louder voice than the abu-bird. He is wearier than can be told and he fares as well as one fares among lions; and when he comes into his house at evening, the going has cut him to pieces.

The weaver in the workshop, he fares more ill than any women. His thighs are upon his belly, and he breathes no air. He plucks lotus flowers from the pond. He gives bread to the doorkeeper that he may suffer him to come into the daylight.

The fletcher does not do well when he goes up into the desert to find flints for arrow-heads. He gives much for his donkey and he gives much for what is in the field. When he sets out on the road and comes into the house in the evening the trip has cut him to pieces.

The cobbler fares exceedingly ill, he begs ever; he bites leather.

The fuller washes upon the river bank, close to the crocodile. This is no peaceful calling in your eyes that would be more tranquil than all callings.

The fowler does not fare well when he looks at the birds in the air. When the passers-by are joined to the heavens, he says, I wish I had a net up there, but he has no such success.

*Let me tell you more, say, about the fisherman;
it goes worst of all for him than any other profession.
Is not his work upon the river where he is mixed with
the crocodile?*

*Listen, there is no profession that is without a
director except the scribe and the scribe is the director.*

*If he knows the books then truth is revealed:
They are good for you. What I now do on the voyage
up to the Residence, I do it for you. A day in school
is very profitable and endures like the mountains.*

Books in papyrus were abundant but not everyone could read. Yet the society sought to make every person a true believer in the cosmology of Kemet and therefore at the temples and in the funerary tombs, it was necessary to have words, sacred words, that could be instruments for conveying images, symbols, and ideas of power. Thus, it was possible that the admonition to read books, to concentrate on learning what was in books, was meant to encourage a massive literacy. Although I am aware of the caste system that existed within the society, it is true that the faculty for reading was not something that could be easily retained within the confines of one caste. Many of the artisans who worked in the temples came from lower castes; however, only the scribes and priest could officiate in the actual inscribing on the walls.

Duauf truly seeks to prepare the student for the world. Every conceivable profession will bring some pleasure and some success, but in the end none will survive like the love of books. His tongue-in-cheek treatment of the occupations makes the point that the love of books is the greatest key to life.

Duauf

CHAPTER TWELVE: AKHENATEN: THE DIVINE IS EVERYWHERE

No ancient Egyptian is any better known than Akhenaten, with the possible exception of Ramses II and Tutankhamen, who both compared in authority and influence. One would, at any rate, place Akhenaten among the top three Egyptian names most recognized by the contemporary public. Whatever one's belief about the efficacy of Akhenaten's movement to modify the indigenous religion of Waset, clearly he was a figure to be reckoned with in the history of the people. He was a vigorous advocate for his position and a true believer in the idea of one god. Whether this was a new development in ancient Egypt or not has often been a question, but what has not been a question is the role played by Akhenaten in the redefining of the role of the pharaoh vis-a-vis the high priests of the state religion.

Akhenaten had been born into the great 18th Dynasty. He had been named Amenhotep IV and slated for the throne of Egypt. While yet a teenager he married the Persian princess, Nefertiti, and there begins the story of his trouble with the established religion.

We do not know exactly where he was educated, but there is no indication that he was taken beyond Egypt. Indeed, there was no reason for him to travel to any other shore for education since in the court of his father, Amenhotep III, he would have been exposed to the best minds of the day.

Amenhotep III moved his court from Memphis to Waset (Thebes) during the latter part of his reign. It was the headquarters for the priests of the sun and perhaps one could have received an education in solar theology from these priests much greater than could ever have been gained in Waset. Yet the education of Amenhotep IV in solar theology was not necessary in any formal sense inasmuch as all Egyptians participated in some form of solar veneration anyway. Ra was the Supreme Deity and was known all over Egypt even if Heliopolis was the central place for the major theologians. Amenhotep IV's uncle, Anen, was a priest of the sun god, but this may have been as one of the ranks of Amen at Karnak, as opposed to some special role as a major theologian.

Modification in religious iconography came with the transformation of Amenhotep IV to Akhenaten. The Parennefer, the overseer of the prophets of God, complained that some had not changed the directions of their offerings to give them to the Disc. The king himself had risen to the position of pharaoh soon after the death of his father, Amenhotep III.

Karnak Temple, a vast complex of religious labyrinths, tekenu, pylons, and corridors to sacred places had been nearly completed by Amenhotep III. This was, of course, many years before the great construction of Seti I, Rameses II, and Tarharka, among other kings. Nevertheless, when Amenhotep IV came to power, he extended the designs of his father, decorated pylons that had remained undecorated, and generally showed himself devoted to the completion of Amenhotep III. Yet already by this time, even with his seeming devotion, Amenhotep IV was beginning to question the religion of his fathers.

One of the things that we know is that early in the second year of his reign he ordered preparation for a jubilee or sed festival, usually reserved for the 30th year of rule. He wanted one to coincide with the third anniversary of his accession to the throne. His chief sculptor, Bek, who had succeeded the chief sculptor, Men, who had directed the sculpturing for his father, was asked to portray the king's musculature, youth, and beauty. Great controversy has arisen among many Egyptologists regarding how Akhenaten looked because of the various ways he was portrayed. Rather than believing that Bek had his workers to portray him as he was, these Egyptologists have contended that Akhenaten's lips were too fleshly, his cheekbones too high, his eyes too slanted, and his neck too slender. On the other hand, Kemetologists, the Afrocentric students of Ancient Kemet, have argued that Akhenaten looked like many other Africans.

Akhenaten's later history blurs as we contemplate his philosophical journey. His name and activities in Waset (Thebes) were so thoroughly obliterated that he has become invisible in the writing of the great narratives of the ancient capital. Without the stelae, tomb paintings, temple decorations, and other records of the nobles of the king's reign, it is impossible to tell a full story. Not only was the name of the king obliterated by Horemhab and other kings who followed but the buildings that we know, from other sources, that he commanded to be built in Karnak, cannot be found. One looks in vain for any trace of the buildings; no fallen columns or facades with the names of the buildings or the king appear in any section of Karnak. We have reached here a cul-de-sac of the king's time at Waset.

Now we can turn our attention to his philosophical problems. When Akhenaten came to power as Amenhotep IV, the most awesome thing about Waset was the presence of Amen. Every king of the 18th Dynasty had piled high offerings to the god and the magnificent temple at Karnak was the beginning of wisdom and the source of all power. It was here that the kings came to be revitalized and to pay homage to Amen who gave them the breath of life and kept their estate in proper balance and harmony. So rich had Karnak become through gifts of goods, animals, and land to the estate of Amen that the god was the principal landowner in all of Upper Egypt. And the temple of Amen, with all of its power, had amassed not only property and wealth in its estate, but also attendants to a degree not seen in any other temple. Amen's house was a complex responsible for a large staff of hundreds of priests. Parochial societies were not always as large and diverse as that of Amen. Indeed, at the Temple

101

of Edfu which was dedicated to Heru, there was a scribe, lector priest, wab priest, prophets, and hour priests of the temple. The staff of the Osiris temple comprised prophets, wab priests, lector priests, and scribes. Occasionally one also finds god's treasurers, regulators of phyle, "he who is over the mysteries," and "overseers of the ergastulum." But by the time of Tuthmoses III, the House of Amen included a sacred staff consisting of prophets, god's fathers, scribes, superintendents of the mysteries, shrine openers, solar-priests, lector priests, assistants, wab priests, mortuary priests, and a large secular staff. Thus, by the second half of the 18th Dynasty the priesthood had become an entrenched occupation where entire families gained their livelihood from the sacred profession.

Amen, "the hidden," was the power of Waset and as a deity he had been given the titles usually reserved for the god-kings of Egypt. He was the king of heaven, risen as Harakhty-Atum, whose physical form is unknown; he was projected as the sovereign of all the gods, prince of princes, and king of Upper and Lower Egypt; and he was master of the cosmos who, like Ptah, transforms himself into an infinite number of forms. Thus, in Waset he was the father of fathers, without equal, infinite, unique, and one who created all things.

One can gather some idea of the situation when Akhenaten confronted Amen, the sole god of the universe, the Ra who shines above all. The fact that he came to reject the advice of the ancient families and chose new administrators to listen to means that he was probably out of touch with those who had ruled in Waset for more than a century. His father, Amenhotep III, obviously gave him no opportunity to learn the proper means of judging the character of others. It is the abruptness of his changes in the structure of the traditional religion that gives his philosophy so much magnetism for those who are drawn to the Amarna Period.

Praise to Aten
Beautiful you rise, O eternal living god!
You are radiant, lovely, powerful,

Your love is great, all-encompassing.
Your rays make all radiant,
Your brightness gives life to hearts,
When you fill the Two Lands with your love.
Revered God who fashioned himself,
Who made every land, created what is in it.
All peoples, herds and flocks,
All trees that grow from soil;
They live when you rise for them,
You are mother and father of all that you made.

When you rise their eyes observe you
As your rays light the whole earth;
Every heart acclaims your sight
When you are risen as their lord.
When you set in the sky's western horizon,
They lie down as if to die,
Their heads covered, their noses stopped,
Until you rise in the sky's eastern horizon
Their arms adore your ka,
As you nourish the hearts by your beauty;
One lives when you cast your rays,
Every land is in festivity.

    The god Aten, from which we get Athena and Athens, had no great mythology and could convey no sense of the awe that one was struck with when in the presence of Amen, for Amen, like Ptah and Atum and Ra, had depth and national reach unknown to Aten. There was no archetype that guided the style attesting to the new god and no words of Aten's power, as far as we can tell, other than the eloquent lyrics of the king himself. There were no great processional temples, no host of priests, and no offerings to the ever changing transformations of the beautiful manifestations of Ra. For this reason, some have called Akhenaten not a theist but an atheist because what he left in the land of Kemet was not a god but a disc, without life and without myth and without mystery, and therefore without longevity.

When one examines the use of the word "Aten," one sees that it is an ancient term that means "disc" and it goes back to the Old Kingdom. During the Old Kingdom this word was used to denote a circular object such as a mirror, cult objects, or balls. It might have also acquired the meaning of "day's disc" meaning the sun in the sky. So when Akhenaten took Aten to be the sole deity he was in effect raising a common deity to the royal and, consequently, universal level.

Amen had long been associated with Ra, as in Amen-Ra. As such, he was the universal deity, a mighty celestial power, who could be invoked for the national good in times of trouble. But Akhenaten perhaps disturbed by the power of the ancient families that were devoted to Amen, sought to minimize the authority of Amen and consequently interjected Aten, as "one who created everything," as the principal deity of his reign and therefore a full-fledged deity.

The first five years of Akhenaten's reign were spent in Waset, but he had laid his plans for the new capital, Akhetaten. Nevertheless, the king pursued his purging of the name of Amen from temples and other official buildings. In fact, he was so eager to pursue his policy that when the time came for inscriptions on the new temples at Akhetaten he commanded that they not refer to Amen but to Aten. Dispatching hundreds of inspectors throughout the country Akhenaten wanted to ensure that the name was eradicated. Thus, in temples, tombs, casual inscriptions, statuary, and any other object that could be written on, he had the name of Amen obliterated and Aten's name substituted. Everywhere they chiseled out the name of Amen and replaced the sacred objects dedicated to him with those made for Aten. People who bore names that ended with Amen were obliged to change them and the king was obliged to protect people who did that. The king led the way by changing his name from Amenhotep meaning "Amen is satisfied," to Akhenaten meaning "effective for the sun disc."

Akhenaten

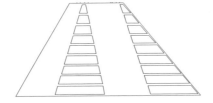

CHAPTER THIRTEEN: AMENEMOPE: ON THE USE OF TIME

Amenemope, the Scribe, son of Kanakht, writes one of the simplest examples of ancient Egyptian ethical philosophy. The Instructions, or Seboyet, often referred to as Wisdom, were written during the 10th century BC and represent the culmination of many ideas found in the long traditions of Egypt. Indeed, there is so much similarity in the book of Proverbs to the Seboyet of Amenemope that some scholars have thought that Solomon was a student of the Egyptians, which, of course, is quite possible, although it is difficult to establish a direct linkage between the Egyptian and Hebrew literatures. Yet one can find it profitable to compare Proverbs 22:17–24 with the Seboyet of Amenemope. Whether there is a direct linkage or not, the older Seboyet must have served in some way as a model for all ancient literatures of the proverbial type. The line in Proverbs 22:20 which says, "Have I not written for you thirty sayings of admonition and knowledge," refers, I believe, to the "thirty" chapters of Amenemope.

In many ways the teachings of Amenemope are like the later Analects of Confucius, not simply because of their humanism but because of their style. As Confucius was later to do in China, Amenemope gave the Egyptian people the wisdom that he had observed in their own behaviors. As a student of human nature and the cosmogonies of Egypt which were from long ago, the philosopher could combine the elements of the natural world with those of the human condition and develop an approach to humanism that is most meaningful to society. His approach, as seen in the Instructions, is direct advice.

The text comes from the British Museum Papyrus 10474. A fragment of the manuscript occurs on a writing tablet in Turin. The date is usually established at the 10th Century BC.

According to the text:

First Chapter:
Give your ears, hear what is said
Allow your heart to understand them.
To let these words come into your heart is worth-while
But to ignore them is damaging.
Let them rest in the middle of your belly
So that they may be a key in your heart.
When there is tornado of words
They shall be an anchoring place for your tongue.
If you spend your time while this is in your heart
You will be successful.
You will find my words a treasury of life,
And you will prosper upon the earth

Second Chapter:
Guard yourself against robbing the oppressed
And against overbearing the physically-challenged.
Stretch not your hand against an old man
Nor steal away the speech of the elders.
Do not allow yourself to be sent on a dangerous errand,
Nor love the one who carries it out.
Do not cry out against the one whom you have
    attacked
Nor answer him on your own behalf.
He who does evil is abandoned by the river banks
And the flood waters sweeps him away.
The North Wind comes so that it may end his hours;

It is joined to the tempest;
The thunder is loud and the crocodiles are wicked.
You impulsive fellow, how are you now?
He is crying out and his voice reaches heaven
Djehuty, establish his crime against him!
So steer that we might bring the wicked man across,
For we shall not act like him—
Lift him up, give your hand;
Leave him in the arm of god;
Fill his stomach with your bread
So that he may be satisfied and be ashamed.
Another good deed in the heart of god

Thirtieth Chapter:
You have seen these thirty chapters:
They entertain; they instruct;
They are the greatest of all books;
They make the ignorant to know,
If they are read out before the ignorant
They will make him clean.
Fill yourself with them, put them in your heart,
And be a man who can interpret them,
Who will interpret them as a teacher.
As for the scribe who is experienced in office
He will find himself worthy to be a courtier
It has come to its end in the writing of Senu,
son of the God's Father Pa-miu.

The evidence that Amenemope uses all of his knowledge of the Egyptian way of life in his teachings is overwhelming in his Seboyet. Indeed, in the Fourth Chapter, he manages to use words and concepts such as *temple, garden, shipyards,* and *burial shroud* in ways that demonstrate his focus on local situations. It was these situations that later became valuable as more universal interpretations.

In the Sixth Chapter, Amenemope writes about boundaries and provides the protocol for how to deal with land disputes in all situations but especially when dealing with widows. Amenemope argues that one should not be greedy in disputes. His instruction says, "better is poverty in the hand of god, than riches in a storehouse" or "better is bread when the heart is happy than riches in sorrow."

He continues this theme, that is, the theme on the dangers of seeking after riches in the Seventh Chapter. "Do not strain to seek excessive riches when your needs are safe and satisfied. If riches are brought to you by robbery they will not spend the night with you."

In the Ninth Chapter, Amenemope claims that one should not associate with evil people nor visit with them in social conversations because you really do not know how they will take the information you share with them. He also counsels, "Preserve your tongue from answering to a superior."

It is not meant here that the superior would become angry but rather there are two separate behaviors that come into play in this section. The first is what happens when you speak to angry or heated persons and the second is a concern about loyalty. Thus, keep your mouth from speaking or answering to a superior because you are the servant of the superior. It is out of respect for the superior that the subordinate defers. This is not meant as an absolute prohibition, but rather to ensure, as in other seboyet, the proper emphasis on loyalty.

Using time wisely is often a most difficult thing for humans to do because we do not know what is more valuable in a given situation. This is why Amenemope's chapters are devoted to establishing priorities in life, for if we have the proper understanding of our purpose, or at least, an understanding that brings the greater happiness to ourselves and our fellows, then our living is not in vain.

Amenemope

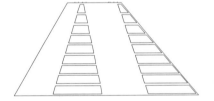

CHAPTER FOURTEEN: THE LIVING WORD OF MAAT

The nature of Maat is to be alive, that is, to be alive in this world or in the other world. Death is truly the avenue from one world to the other. So to live in Maat is to live the living word, the *ankh mdw*. It becomes the only path to *ankh neheh*, that is, life eternal. This is the great quest of the person who seeks to live by the standards established in the First Occasion. Maat was the cohesive element that made the First Occasion the symbolic representation of victory over evil.

That the word could be living is the great mystery of Maat. One does not find the word merely as a dead artifact or as a lifeless abstraction; it is active, dynamic, and alive in the everyday lives of humans at work, play, and worship. How I approach each day, that is, how I come to acknowledge my existence in the presence of the divine, which is another name for the unknown, is an aspect of Maat. I come to the day searching for ways to establish harmony, justice, righteousness, balance, and reciprocity. Indeed, I am what I am and who I am by virtue of my Maatic quest. If I do not seek Maat I am no more than a piece of trash tossed about by the wind! It is Maat that gives me focus, organizes my thoughts, and governs my actions.

Since Maat was intrinsic to the First Occasion it is the great barrier to the descent into Nun, or Chaos. Like someone holding a wall of respect and honor against the raging powers of disrespect and dishonor on the other side, the Maatic person becomes heroic in the quest. Maat is more than an idea that is being pursued, Maat is a substance that can be apprehended. This is why the ancients would sometime say that "I eat Maat" or "Maat is my daily refreshment." Can one live without water? In the ancient world Maat was always represented as a goddess and Atum was encouraged by the god Nun to "kiss your daughter Maat, let her be like oxygen to your nose that you may live!"

What are the conditions of stability, eternal life, and peace? One must do Maat and keep Maat in the heart in order to be fully human.

What is Maat but the right ordering of the universe during the first time? In many ways the Greeks, particularly Plato, found the Egyptian idea useful for the area of the first existence of the Platonic ideal. Jeremy Naydler in *Temple of the Cosmos* argues that the first time is the realm of the metaphysical where symbolic images and myths are conceived.

However, the ancient Africans believed that the earliest time, indeed, the first time, was a period of perfection prior to chaos. It is possible that one can perceive this time as a one time phenomenon, but I am inclined to see it as the ancients saw it—as a recurring moment. We all experience the first time and sometimes we experience it several times a day. This is the great mystery of living and indeed of dying.

Maat represented as a goddess who was the daughter of the Almighty Atum-Ra. Indeed, as the daughter of Atum-Ra, Maat was made of the same substance as the Almighty. Thus, her universal attributes of justice, order, righteousness, harmony, balance, and reciprocity made her part of the divine ordering of the universe. When the primeval waters of Nun were subsumed under the divine power of the emanating Maat, order overcame chaos, harmony ruled over disharmony, and the entire universe was just. This is the continuing ritual drama of the first time.

In the ancient text, Maat is usually depicted as a winged goddess with an ostrich feather in her hair and an ankh in her hand. The ostrich feather in her hair is similar to the depiction of the feather in the hair of Shu. Nun is recorded as admonishing Atum, the Almighty, with these words about Maat.

Kiss your daughter Maat,
put her to your nose,
that your heart may live,
for she will not be far from you;
Maat is your daughter
and your son is Shu whose name lives.
Eat of your daugher Maat;
it is your son Shu who will raise you up.

The overwhelming nature of Maat as a part of our existence is recorded in this ancient text. For us to kiss Maat, put her to our nose where she becomes our oxygen so that our heart may live, means that there is no life without Maat. Eat of Maat, make Maat a part of your daily undertaking, and understand that Maat will raise you up through Shu. This is powerful stuff. The Christians say, God is within you; the Africans said it a long time ago. But to get God in you, one must eat, drink, and sleep Maat.

What strikes me is the absolute impossibility of living effectively without Maat. There can be no genuine human relations without the persistent challenge of discovering in all aspects of life the over-arching principle of Maat. To ask, for instance, what are your principles? One should hope to hear in response that one's principles are all authentically grounded in the concepts that make up the idea of Maat. In this way Maat lives.

Consider how easy it is for us to have the idea that money would make us happy, indeed secure. The pursuit of money becomes the aim of life and once money is attained, emptiness remains. How can an artist make beautiful art and then sell it?

Here was a highly civilized people, who created organized systems of managing differences, the prosecution of justice, and response to the environment, and yet Kemet did not use gold or silver coins as money. They possessed gold, and during some periods e.g., the reigns of Mentuhotep I, Tuthmoses III, Amenhotep III, and Ramses II, they seemed to have lots of gold, but even then they did not make money the cornerstone of their society, nor did they export a money culture because they did not use gold as a means of exchange. Gold was used in all forms of royal and sacerdotal decorations, such as chairs, palanquins, staffs, and fabrics, but it was not considered money. There were no gold coins, for example.

However, there was always Maat and the person who could best demonstrate in his or her life its presence was considered a good and decent person. Although we are the inheritors of a tradition of respect, courtesy, justice, propriety, and reciprocity, we have not fully understood Maat. In this new millennium, we must reclaim this philosophy inherited from the dawn of human consciousness.

Finally, we have not fully explored all the ways the ancient philosophers brought the truth to their societies. They were deeply committed to a spiritual affirmation based on their relationship with the forces and energies of the deities. Learning how to hold back chaos in society was a revered course of study. This was what the philosophers specialized in and consequently, as the first philosophers in the world, they inspired a sense of wonder at the universe, human relations, and eternity. The practice of the African philosophers along the Nile was a practice of maintaining Maat in every aspect of life. If we could only learn from them the value of harmony, balance, and righteousness, we would be on our own way toward a revival of the spirit of human victory.

GLOSSARY OF USEFUL TERMS

Akh—Alongside the ka and the ba, one of the three major constituents of human identity. Akh refers to the essence of a person's immortality that leaves the body at death to join the stars. The akh was represented by the crested ibis.

Ba—Alongside the ka and the akh, one of the three major constituents of human identity. The ba was present at the ceremonial weighing of the owner's heart after death. It was symbolically represented as a human-headed bird flying between the living and dead.

Coffin Texts—Inscribed on coffins and sarcophagi, these were a collection of more than a thousand different spiritual sayings meant to safely guide the deceased through the afterworld.

Dromos—Processional way that led to and from the temples.

Execration Texts—These texts were usually written on pottery and contained a list of enemies of the Kemetic people, usually foreign princes and kings.

Golden Horus Name—One of the five elements making up the classic royal titulary.

Hieroglyphics—Greek word for sacred carved letters.

Horus Name—The first and earliest recorded epithet in the written sequence of the king's name, usually found in the serekh.

Hyksos (Hekaw Khasut)—Asiatics who infiltrated Egypt during the Middle Kingdom and became rulers in Lower Egypt (Northern Egypt), from 1750–1550BC.

Hypostyle Hall—Massive columned hall at the front of the temple which was considered symbolic of the primeval swamp.

Ipet-Isut—The most esteemed of places was the original central area of the Temple of Amen at Karnak, stretching from the Festival Hall of Tuthmoses III to the fourth pylon. Later it became the term used for Karnak itself.

Ka—One of the three major constituents of human identity, with the ba and the akh, that came into being at the same time as the body, of which it was the life-force or personality. After death it was the ka which moved through the false door between the tomb and chapel to consume the offering.

Maat—The aim of Kemetic society was the maintenance of Maat. Represented as a goddess, Maat constituted order, balance, harmony, justice, righteousness, and reciprocity; in fact, it was the entire principle of the equilibrium of society.

Nomen—The royal birth name, usually the second name written in the titulary of a king, accompanied by the phrase, sa Ra, that is, Son of God.

Pyramid Texts—A collection of powerful sayings carved on the internal walls of pyramids from the time of Wenis until the 8th Dynasty (2470– 2200BC). The texts concern the safe passage of the king through the afterworld. The corpus of the Pyramid Texts and the subsequent Coffin Texts formed the basis for the *Book of the Dead.*

Two Ladies Name—One of the five titularies of the king. The Two Ladies were the vulture-goddess Nekhbet and the cobra-goddess Wadjet, representing Upper and Lower Egypt, respectively.

A KEMETIC CHRONOLOGY

Foundation of the Empire
(1st Dynasty 3500–2980 BC)
Narmer (Menes)
Aha
Djer
Den
Semerkhet
Qaa

(2nd Dynasty 2980–2686 BC)
Hotepsekhemwi
Nynetjer
Peribsen
Khasekhemwi

First Golden Period
(3rd Dynasty 2686–2613 BC)
Sanakhte
Zoser
Sekhemket
Huni

(4th Dynasty 2613–2494 BC)
Sneferu
Khufu
Khafre
Menkaure

(5th Dynasty 2494–2345 BC)
Userkofi

Sahure
Nyuserre
Unas

(6th Dynasty 2345–2181 BC)
Teti
Pepi I
Merenre
Pepi II

First Period of Instability
This was the time of the first period of political instability which lasted from 2181 to about 2133 BC. The period included the 7th to 10th dynasties.

Second Golden Period
(11th Dynasty 2133–1991 BC)
Mentuhotep I
Inyotef I-III
Mentuhotep II-IV

(12th Dynasty 1991–1786 BC)
Amenemet I
Senursert I
Senursert II
Amenemet III

(13th Dynasty 1786–1633 BC)
Sebekhotep III
Neferhotep

Second Period of Instability
A second period of political unrest in which Kemet was governed in part by the Asiatic Hyksos occurred. The 14th, 15th, 16th, and 17th dynasties consisted of intermittent rule by Hyksos and indigenous rulers.

New Kingdom
(18th Dynasty 1567–1320 BC)
Amosis
Amenhotep
Tuthmoses I
Tuthmoses II
Hatshepsut
Tuthmoses III
Amenhotep II
Tuthmoses IV
Amenhotep III
Amenhotep IV (Akhenaten)
Smenkhkare
Tutankhamen
Ay
Horemhab

(19th Dynasty 1320–1200 BC)
Rameses I
Seti I
Rameses II
Merneptah
Amen-meset
Seti II

(20th Dynasty 1200–1085 BC)
Sethnakhte
Rameses III
Rameses IV-XI

Third Period of Instability
The third great period of political instability occurred between 1085 and 750 BC. This was a time of family and clan rivalries, ethnic jealousies, political disorganization in foreign policy, and lack of vision.

Third Golden Period
(25th Dynasty 750–656 BC)
Piankhi
Shabaka
Taharka
Shabataka

The Decline of the Great Kingdom
(26th, 27th, 28th, 29th,and 30th Dynasties 656–50 BC)
Psammetichus I
Necho II
Apries
Amasis

The 27th Dynasty was an Assyrian dynasty. There were a couple of indigenous dynasties after that, and then in 333 BC, the Greeks conquered Egypt under Alexander and instituted the Ptolemaic Period that lasted until Roman conquest. The Romans were eventually defeated in 641 AD by the Arabs who had been asked by the indigenous people to come in and help throw off the invaders.

REFERENCES

Primary Philosophical Texts and Translations

Akhenaten, "Hymns to Aten," Author's Translation. Copy can be found in Miriam Lichtheim, *Ancient Egyptian Literature,* Vol. II, Berkeley: University of California Press, 1975. Found originally on the West Wall, 13 columns, in the Tomb of Ay, there are more than twenty different translations of the hymns.

Ptahhotep, "Moral Teachings" Originally from the Papyrus Prisse of the Bibliotheque Nacionale. My translation is based on two versions, B. Gunn's translations in *The Instruction of Ptah-hotep* and the Instruction of Kagemni: in Isaac Myers' *The Oldest Books in the World.* London: Kegan Paul, French, 1900. Another translation can be found in Asa Hilliard, Larry Williams, and Nia Damali's *The Teachings of Ptahhotep,* Atlanta: Blackwood press, 1987.

Kagemni, originally translated from the Papyrus Prisse by B. Gunn. English updated by the author. A copy of this text was translated by Isaac Myers in *The Oldest Books in the World.* London: Kegan Paul, French, 1900.

Amenemope, "Instructions for Well Being," The Author's translation relies on E. A. Budge, *The Teachings of Amen-em-apt, Son of Kane*kht. London, 1924, and F. Griffith, *Journal of Egyptian Archaeology,* 12, 1926, pp. 191-231.

All other works cited are in the public domain and are found in numerous sources.

SELECTED REFERENCES

Aldred, Cyril. *The Egyptians.* London, Thames & Hudson, 1984

Aldred, Cyril. *Akhenaten: King of Egypt.* London, Thames & Hudson, 1988.

Amin, M. A. Ancient Trade Routes Between Egypt and the Sudan, 4000 to 700 BC, SNR (Sudan Notes and Records), 51, 23–40.

Asante, Molefi and Abu Abarry, eds. *The African Intellectual Heritage.* Philadelphia: Temple University Press, 1996.

Asante, Molefi Kete. *Kemet, Afrocentricity and Knowledge.* Trenton: Africa World Press, 1990.

Austin, M. M. *Greece and Egypt in the Archaic Age.* Cambridge: Cambridge University Press, 1970.

Bell, Barbara. "The Dark Ages in Ancient History I: The First Dark Age in Egypt," American Journal of Archaeology, 75, 1–26.

Bernal, Martin. *Black Athena.* New Brunswick: Rutgers University Press, 1987.

Bleiberg, Edward. "Historical Texts as Political Propaganda During the New Kingdom," BES (Bulletin of Egyptological Seminar) 7, 5–14.

Browder, Anthony. *Nile Valley Contributions to Civilization.* Washington: Karmaic Institute, 1988.

Brugsch, H. *Materiaux pour le Calendrier des Anciens Egyptiens,* p. 80

Clark, R. T. Rundle. *Myth and Symbol in Ancient Egypt.* London: Thames and Hudson, 1978.

Diop, Cheikh Anta. *The African Origin of Civilization.* New York: Lawrence Hill, 1974.

Diop, Cheikh Anta. *Civilization or Barbarism.* New York: Lawrence Hill, 1988.

Faulkner, R. O. *The Coffin Texts.* Warminster: Aris and Phillips, 1978.

Froidefond, Christian. "Le mirage egyptien dans la litterature grecque, d'Homere a Aristote." Aix-en-Provence, 1971.

Gardiner, Sir A. *Egyptian Grammar.* Oxford: Ashmolean Museum, 1994.

Giedeon, S. *La naissance de l'architecture.* Brussels, 1966.

Hilliard, Constance. *Intellectual Traditions of Pre-Colonial Africa.* Boston: McGraw Hill, 1997.

James, George G. M. *Stolen Legacy.* Trenton: Africa World Press, 1990.

Karenga, Maulana. *Introduction to Black Studies.* Los Angeles: University of Sankore Press, 1995.

Lehman, Cynthia. *SDM MDW PN M WRT MAAT: A Classical Kemetic Foundation for the Study of African Oratory,* unpublished dissertation, Temple University, 1997.

Lichtheim, M. *Ancient Egyptian Literature.* Berkeley: University of California, 1961.

Meyers, Isaac. *The Oldest Books in the World.* London: Kegan Paul, 1900.

Naydler, Jeremy. *The Temple of the Cosmos.* New York: Inner Traditions, 1994.

Obenga, Theophile. *African Philosophy in the Context of World History.* Princeton: Sungai Books, 1997.

Petrie, W. M. F. "Ceremonial Slate Palettes," British School of Egypt Archaeology. 66, 1953.

Poe, Richard. *Black Spark, White Fire.* New York: Prima, 1997.

Posener, Georges. "Les Asiatiques en Egypte sous les 12 et 13 dynasties." Syria 34, 145–163, 1957.

Pritchard, James B. *Ancient Near Eastern Texts Relating to the Old Testament.* Princeton: Princeton University Press, 1955.

Ridley, R. T. "The Discovery of the Pyramid Texts," Zeitscrift fur Agyptische Sprache Und Altertumskunde, 110, 74–80.

Williams, Chancellor. *The Destruction of Black Civilization. Great Issues of a Race from 4500 BC to 2000 AD.* Chicago: Third World Press, 1987.